WE STILL KISS

WE STILL
KISS

DR. JAMES B. RICHARDS

**WHITAKER
HOUSE**

WE STILL KISS

Impact Ministries
3300 N. Broad Place SW
Huntsville, AL 35805
256.536.9402 • Fax: 256.536.4530

ISBN: 0-88368-752-6
Printed in the United States of America
© 2002 by Dr. James B. Richards

Whitaker House
30 Hunt Valley Circle
New Kensington, PA 15068
visit our web site: www.whitakerhouse.com

Library of Congress Cataloging-in-Publication Data

Richards, James B. (James Burton), 1951–
  We still kiss / James B. Richards.
    p. cm.
Includes bibliographical references.
  ISBN 0-88368-752-6 (pbk. : alk. paper)
  1. Marriage—Religious aspects—Christianity. 2. Love—Religious aspects—Christianity. 3. Intimacy (Psychology)—Religious aspects—Christianity. I. Title.
  BV835 .R525 2002
  261.8' 35—dc21

2002008239

1 2 3 4 5 6 7 8 9 10 11 / 09 08 07 06 05 04 03 02

Dedication

I dedicate this book to my five daughters, Tonya, Christy, Amy, Summer, and Julie. You have been so patient with me as I have "grown up" and learned how to love. I have written this book for you! I pray that you can find the love that Brenda and I have without all the mistakes and pain.

I love you.

—Dad

Contents

Introduction

Our quality of life is determined by our quality of love. The ability to have meaningful, loving relationships is the single most important factor for happiness. Recent studies indicate that our capacity for love is a major factor in health and longevity. Jesus listed it as the only true proof of spiritual growth, and Paul said that love from a pure heart was the goal of all instruction.

Everyone wants love. It is essential for every area of life, yet it seems that few of us have the tools to find this "elixir of life." *We Still Kiss* is a book that is born out of the real-life struggles of my own marriage. It reveals the biblical secrets that have made a seemingly impossible relationship not only survive but also flourish in the face of every imaginable obstacle. After more than twenty years of raising kids, several life-threatening illnesses, dire poverty, and the continual demands of a growing ministry, we still kiss, and we're still passionately in love.

Not only will every chapter of this book open doors to biblical insight, but each will also give you practical examples and personal stories that model the underlying principles. At the end of every chapter, you will be given questions or steps that you can take to bring the capacity for love into your relationship.

Love is not a pit that you accidentally fall into. It is not a destination! It is not a one-time decision. It is an interactive, dynamic interplay. It is a never-ending journey that is renewed daily. The moment you stop paying attention to it, love begins to slip from you. It will require more of you than any other area of life. But it will give back to you a thousand times more than you will ever give.

You can have a life of love, romance, and passion that never ends. Brenda and I walked into a store a few days ago, and the manager said, "I just have to ask, are you two newlyweds?" "No, we've been married over twenty years," was Brenda's reply. "Why do you ask?" "You just look so happy together. Everybody here talks about it." No matter where you are in your relationship, you can apply these realities and find the keys to love and romance.

Chapter 1

The Story of Us

Chapter 1

The Story of Us

I sat in a swing on the playground across from our apartment. The sun was sinking behind the horizon, leaving the sky a dark gray abyss that seemed to reflect my life. The red-streaked clouds lowering in the distance were like the unhealed scars in my soul, left by the years of pain. I guess every married couple has difficult times that seem never to end—the insurmountable obstacles, the eternal impasse! But how could I be here again?

I thought I had found true love. I thought that the life of struggling with rejection and abandonment was over. But like the ravenous lions that lie in the tall grass and wait for the defenseless gazelle to stray into their grip of death, so are the unresolved issues of our past. They lie in wait for our blood! At the moment of greatest weakness, they rise up to violently steal what is left of our lives.

After I had prayed, cried, and wiped away the tears, I determined that I would not let the past dictate my future. Regardless of my personal failure, the history of dysfunction, and the shame of moral and personal failure, I would not give up. If God's Word were true, then no matter where I was, no matter how far over the edge my life was, if I wanted to be recovered, I could.

I had backslidden. After a series of major operations, it was questionable if I would live. Years of medical treatment with no insurance had left me financially devastated. I barely had enough money to make ends meet. My kids were wearing old clothes. We rarely had enough groceries, and I was being sued. But none of that really mattered very much! What mattered was that I was in love, and I wondered if our marriage would survive.

I pulled myself together, went back in the apartment, and looked at Brenda, my wife, the woman I loved. I never told her my fears or the deep pain I was experiencing. Words would not solve the problem. There were no formulas or magic cures. And like all "life problems," there was no one thing that caused them, and there was no one solution to fix them. Nevertheless, my goal was clear: all I wanted was a marriage that worked, a relationship that did not end in disappointment.

> If God's Word is true, then no matter where you are, no matter how far over the edge your life is, if you want to be recovered, you can.

The Decision That Changed Everything

When I think back to that bleak moment in my past, it seems more like a tragic novel that became so sad I had to lay it down. The end seemed obvious, the outcome predictable. What had happened before would happen again, and the cycle would go on.

Unlike "real life," though, that is not how my story ends! It has been more than twenty years since that horrible night. And although this story is actually a work in progress, it has been a blissful life with a near fairy-tale ending. The two most unlikely candidates for happiness find the elixir of love and happiness and share their treasure with people all over the world. That is the story of us!

One night about two years after my "night of decision," a man sat at my kitchen table. He had been devastated by a painful divorce. For several years this one-time family man ran the clubs of Huntsville, Alabama, trying to drink and fornicate his sorrow away. It didn't work. It only served to multiply his pain and shame.

This man looked me in the eye and said, "I had given up on God. And I had given up on marriage. But I have seen what your and Brenda's marriage has become. I've seen the happiness you have in this home. If God can do that for you, He can do it for me." We prayed, and he gave his life to Jesus as Lord. I eventually had the privilege of performing his wedding when he discovered love after destruction. That story has been repeated numerous times since! The marriage that shouldn't have made it has become a testimony to God's love and grace for many.

I don't believe there is a more empowering decision than deciding to love people.

I would be lying if I told you that one revelation, one experience, or one night of prayer turned my whole world around. It didn't! But one *decision* did. I determined that I would know God's love for myself, and I committed that I would walk in that love. I made it my life's goal that the people in my life would encounter the love of God through me.

That one decision was like the ignition of a rocket engine. When a rocket engine ignites, it creates enough thrust in about eight minutes to propel a space vehicle so powerfully that it will coast to the moon, to Mars, and, according to recent news reports, to the edge of our solar system. I don't believe there is a more empowering decision that any human being can make—other than surrendering your life to the Lordship of Jesus—than deciding to love people.

Come with Us...

I want to take you on a journey with Brenda and me. I want you to join us on an adventure of love and romance that will endure time, transcend your past, heal your wounds, and satisfy your deepest longings. As I write, the words of a song sung by Celine Dion come to my mind: "We're heading for something, somewhere I've never been. Sometimes I am frightened but I'm ready to learn of the power of love."[1] Are you ready to go where you've never been? It will be a journey you will never regret!

Don't let fear hold you back. Don't let the past dictate your future. God is a God of love, and if you will follow Him, He will lead you into a life and a marriage that overflows with love and romance. The number one testimony I get from people who are exposed to the influence of our ministry is that they fall in love with God and with the people in their lives. I want to share with you some of the "elixir" that makes this happen.

Brenda and I have a relationship that people envy. After years of struggles over children, incredible financial ruin, several life-threatening illnesses, and a host of incredible challenges, we are so deeply in love. We still melt at each other's touch. We long for one another when we are apart. We are best friends. We are passionate lovers, and, after all these years and all these storms, we still kiss.

---

[1] Gunther Meade, Candy DeRouge, Jennifer Rush, Mary Susan Applegate, "The Power of Love," performed by Celine Dion. Sony Music Canada Inc., 1993. *The Colour of My Love*. Compact disc.

Chapter 2

Overcoming Your Beginning

Chapter 2

Overcoming Your Beginning

You can't go on with your future if you're stuck in the past. Far too many couples never get on with their relationship because they are questioning its beginning. In an ideal world we would all do things right the first time. However, very few of us do.

Our church here in Huntsville, Alabama, is very active in reaching into the "real world." Nearly everyone who walks through our doors has been married more than once, some as many as eight times. Some national statistics indicate that a little more than half of all believers have been divorced and are struggling with the shame of starting over. Personally, I can't remember the last time I counseled a couple who had not engaged in premarital sex. Many young people have had bisexual experiences. And the number of women who have had abortions is staggering. In short, the number of Christians who violate the guidelines for dating and marriage are just as high as the number of non-Christians.

Because of the idealistic legalism that is presented by the church, people feel that God cannot bless them if they did not do everything "right." We recently had a woman who had been raped call our partner relations department.

She had been taught that because of what had happened, she was an unclean vessel and God could never use her. This type of religious thinking does nothing to solve the problem. It only adds to the years of pain and shame.

So, because we did not have the perfect start, we unfortunately determine that we can't have a perfect ending. It is true that a good start can help us avoid a lot of pain. But very few relationships begin as they should. Even if they do, that is no guarantee they will grow into wonderful relationships. We have to always press forward. As the apostle Paul, who was responsible for murder, said, *"Forgetting those things which are behind, and reaching forth unto those things which are before, I press toward the mark for the prize of the high calling of God in Christ Jesus"* (Philippians 3:13–14).

That might be easier said than done. Most of us have so many hurts, fears, and insecurities that drive us, especially when it comes to dating and marriage. For example, I was from a poor family, so I didn't have the money to buy the "in" clothes. Do you know how hard that is for a teenager? The first car I ever owned was old and ugly. The list of teenage embarrassments seems endless. Many of us have unresolved childhood issues like these that affect our confidence. Our issues drive us to all manner of compromise. Our insecurities make us blind. Our loneliness makes us settle for much less than we could have.

Speaking of compromises, when I began dating I would date almost anyone who was interested. Sometimes I didn't even like the person I was dating. I was with her only because my ego needed a girlfriend to make me feel good about myself.

I had a friend who wanted to date a certain girl. Her father would only let her double date, so my friend asked me to go on a blind date with her best friend. I reluctantly agreed to go. The girl was nice, but she was too young for me. She was not someone I would have dated.

After our double date, my friend called this girl and told her that I was too shy to call and ask, so he was calling in my place to ask if she wanted to go steady with me. I guess she was excited to date someone older, and the next thing I knew, I was going steady. I went to her house to break up with her, but I couldn't do it. So for a few months I dated a girl I didn't even like just because she was interested in me and I was too insecure to do anything about it.

The list of compromises is endless, and as we grow older they grow in magnitude. Most people wake up one day and wonder who it is they really married and why. An incredible number of people actually give up on their marriage at that point. They may go through the motions—feed the kids, attend school functions, buy an anniversary gift, even reluctantly have sex. But it is not the life they wanted. It is not even the life they willingly chose! It is the life that happened to them while they struggled with their insecurities.

I can't tell you how many young women have come to me who had gotten pregnant by a man they didn't want to marry. Sometimes it would be by someone they didn't even like. I used to wonder why someone would even have sex with a person he or she didn't like. I finally realized that for some people it is easier to have sex with a person they don't like than it is to be alone and face the feeling of rejection and loneliness.

Move out of the Past and into the Now

So the idealist would have you believe that if you did not begin your relationship "just right," God could never bless it. Nothing could be further from the truth. You see, God is a right-now God. He is the I Am. All that He is and does is in the now. That is why He is called "The Great I Am," not "The Great I Was." The Bible says in 2 Corinthians 6:2 that now, *today*, is the day of salvation. Regardless of what your yesterday was, His mercies are renewed every morning—and so are your opportunities to experience a new quality of life and relationship. As someone has said, "Though no one can go back and make a brand-new start, anyone can start from now and make a brand-new ending."

Many couples have come to cherish these words nestled in the genealogy of Jesus in Matthew 1:6: *"David was the father of Solomon, whose mother had been Uriah's wife"* (NIV). God made sure that we would forever remember the imperfection of one of His beloved servants. Through this, we see His ability to recover and restore beyond our wildest dreams. He inspired Matthew to remind the people that Solomon was the son of a relationship that began in adultery, deceit, and murder. Yet David went on to be one of the greatest leaders in all history.

> Though no one can go back and make a brand-new start, anyone can start from now and make a brand-new ending.

I once heard a story of a couple who, on the night before their wedding, was called by a well-known preacher. They were in the midst of their rehearsal party. It was the height of the celebration prior to the marriage. Both of their families were there. The preacher called to tell them that God could not bless their wedding because of the groom's past. The preacher, who caused them to cancel their wedding, often touted this story as if it were a crowning moment of successful ministry. Nothing could be further from the truth. All that was accomplished was the destruction of a relationship between two people who could have moved on with their lives and overcome a failed past!

If David had been influenced by a religious thinker such as this well-known pastor, he would have resigned as king of Israel. He would have put Bathsheba away. They both would have spent their lives in shame and degradation and become stuck in an unresolvable past. But even more crucial is the fact that the bloodline of Jesus would have been lost, and man would have raced into eternity without a Savior.

Although David had to work through his personal issues of sin and failure, he did not live the rest of his days in the defeat of that sin. No, he dealt with his sin and moved into the now! Too often we linger in the dark annals of past history, refusing to walk in the light of renewal for fear that the light will only magnify the utter wickedness of our past sin.

Jesus' finished work qualifies me for the blessings of God.

David loved Bathsheba, and through her our very salvation was brought to planet Earth. There were surely those who held contempt in their hearts for David and Bathsheba. I am sure their past had an unpleasant effect on their relationship; they may have forever had to work through issues of shame. Yet through this relationship that began in such wickedness came Solomon, the wisest man of God who ever lived—and ultimately Jesus, the Savior of the world.

I could look to my past and quickly find hundreds of sins or failures that would disqualify me for success in ministry, life, and marriage. But my past is not the reason God blesses me. You see, it is *Jesus'* finished work that qualifies me for the blessings of God.

After spending a year out of ministry and reluctantly allowing God to draw me back, we began reaching into the nations of the world. Since then I've seen many people saved and influenced because of the Gospel message I share. One day I received a call from an old friend. In the conversation he said, "I wondered about you and Brenda getting married. But it is clear that you did the right thing; otherwise God's blessings would not be upon you as they are today!" I quickly replied, "Brenda and I didn't do everything right. We made as many mistakes as you can imagine. God is not blessing us because we did everything right; God is blessing us because we have accepted forgiveness through the Lord Jesus. We have entrusted our lives to God, and we have moved on."

> God's mercies are renewed every morning—and so are your opportunities to experience a new quality of life in your marriage.

It's Not about Fairness, But Forgiveness

This incredible story of David and Bathsheba shatters the idealists' model of God and marriage. Many would cry, "But, God, this is not fair." And I would be the first to agree. David and Bathsheba sinned, yes. But they were redeemed from their sin. God is no different now than He was then. However your marriage began, it can be redeemed. You see, He never gives us what we deserve. He gives us what Jesus deserves. The question is, will we look to our lives and trust in our merits, or will we look to Jesus and trust in His merit?

The very heart of the New Covenant is nestled in unmerited favor. This is a covenant of promise, not of works. Romans 4:6–8 says,

> *David says the same thing when he speaks of the blessedness of the man to whom God credits righteousness apart from*

works: "Blessed are they whose transgressions are forgiven, whose sins are covered. Blessed is the man whose sin the Lord will never count against him." (NIV)

David's personal experience with sin and failure let him know that he did not want what his actions deserved. He appealed to the depths of God's mercy and then moved on with his life. However, in order for him to move on with his life, he had to move on with his relationship with Bathsheba. Regardless of his past failures, he had to make the relationship godly from the day of his repentance forward. He had to move into "the now"!

You have the same choice. You can trust God with the failure of your past, or you can live in the agony of shame and shortcomings. Humility is not when you hang your head down and act like a nobody. True humility is when you surrender your will, your point of view, to God and accept His will and point of view. God's point of view is that you are righteous in Jesus. His will is that you stand up today and walk in that righteousness. Don't use yesterday's failure as an excuse for today's sin. Don't reject God's mercy and grace.

> True humility is when you surrender your will, your point of view, to God and accept His will and His point of view.

Jesus came to free us from what we deserved and to qualify us to receive what God wanted us to have. *"Giving thanks to the Father who has qualified us to be partakers of the inheritance of the saints in the light"* (Colossians 1:12 NKJV). He qualified us to receive all the love of God, whether we deserve it or not. That way, the promise would be sure for everyone. No one would be left out! So even if you started wrong, you do not have to be left out. You are not disqualified from the promises of happiness because of your past.

Your shame about how you dated, about the beginning of your relationship, is buried. It is forgiven and forgotten. All your immorality, abortion, or perversion is washed away by the blood of Jesus. You do no service to God, your mate, or your family by holding on to that shame. Suffering in shame is not a sacrifice to God. It is a commitment to unbelief. It is a refusal to accept the mercy of God. Glorify God by freeing yourself from the shame of the past and moving on to a loving relationship.

No matter how you started, you must commit yourself to today and the future. Before you read another chapter, stop and pray. Make a conscious decision to let go of the past. Say aloud that you release the past. Tell God that you accept His forgiveness in Jesus. Thank Him that sins from the beginning of your relationship or from your past have no control over your life today. Whatever the start of your marriage was like, it can't be any worse than adultery and murder. God wants you to be happy. He wants your relationship to be a testimony to His love and forgiveness.

Chapter 3

First Things First

Chapter 3

First Things First

Someone has said, "The most important thing is to find out what is the most important thing." I couldn't agree more. We exert an incredible amount of sincere effort into things that do not accomplish our goals or fulfill our desires. Our problem is not always a lack of effort, but rather putting that effort into something that does not produce a desired result. In Isaiah 55:2, God presents this powerful principle of "don't put your effort in the wrong place": *"Why do you spend money for what is not bread, and your wages for what does not satisfy? Listen carefully to Me, and eat what is good, and let your soul delight itself in abundance"* (NKJV).

Most people will not waste their lives because they do nothing. They will waste their lives because they put their efforts in the wrong places.

Put Your Effort into God's Way

Although this verse is obviously talking about our relationship with God, the principle applies to every area of life. It is essential at this point that we determine what are the most important things. First of all, God's Word teaches us that we are created in His likeness and image. As such, we are social, emotional, relationship-oriented beings. Our quality of life is directly related to the quality of our relationships—our relationship with God and our relationship with people. We are not "designed" by our Creator to find true fulfillment in ownership, control, power, or any other substitutes. Thus our quality of life is the quality of our relationships.

When God's Word talks about the "proof of spirituality," we see that walking in love and having meaningful relationships is the only real proof. Now, we live in a day when all manner of substitutes have become socially acceptable. For the carnal person, the pursuit of wealth, success, and prestige may be what is most important. For the pseudo-spiritual, the most important thing may be spiritual gifts, a great ministry, or even great spiritual experiences.

We are social, emotional, relationship-oriented beings.

None of these things are wrong in and of themselves, but the moment they become the "first thing" in your life, you are headed down a path that will never lead to fulfillment, peace, or satisfaction. The most important thing, according to Jesus, is to love God with your whole heart and to love your neighbor as yourself. The ability to have loving relationships is the epitome of a great life. Loving relationships are the seat of satisfaction. All else is a substitute that offers false hope and only delivers disappointment.

God's wisdom warns of the emotional destruction that comes from disappointment. *"Hope deferred maketh the heart sick"* (Proverbs 13:12). There are many "heartsick" people who truly believed their pursuits would make them happy. Too many heartsick people have spent their lives on *"what does not satisfy"* (Isaiah 55:2 NKJV). The end of that life is bitterness, anger, emptiness, and loneliness. To spend their lives trying to obtain yet never really reaching the desired results is a root of bitterness for many.

Sadly, some of the most disappointed people are those who are really trying to have good relationships. Remember, the problem is not lack of effort but what the effort is going to. Either they do not understand or they do not trust God's principles of relationship.

For years I labored under an idealistic, male chauvinist paradigm that made a loving, healthy relationship impossible. I could take control, but I could never experience real love. The ego boost of control pales in comparison to the rewards of true love. In early relationships I could get women to do what I wanted. I could use guilt, manipulation, intimidation, obligation, or even beguilement. But when I got what I wanted, it never truly satisfied my soul. It was like eating food that was sweet to taste but bitter in the stomach.

Too often those vain pursuits look almost like the real pursuit of relationships. But without a proper understanding and experience of love, complete satisfaction will never be found. The closer we get to reality without really finding it, the more deceitful and potentially deadly the substitute can be. Trying to get someone to love us, searching to find acceptance, getting someone to meet our needs, having some significant other in our lives—all of these may be important factors, but they are actually deadly, disappointing substitutes that make the heart sick. We've put our efforts in the wrong place.

All of these "relationships" can be sought and developed from a purely self-centered motivation. We can manipulate people into saying the right things; we can make people so

afraid that they "act the part"; we can use others to meet our needs. Regardless of how much it looks like real love, it will never meet our real needs until it is real love. Instead, all of these efforts serve to push true love and romance—the kind that satisfies—further from our reach.

The news recently reported a pharmacist who allegedly watered down cancer drugs. Although there was some of the "real thing" in the prescription, there was evidently not enough to cure the sickness. So it is with these deadly substitutes. They are so close to the real thing that we can't tell the difference. They deceive us into thinking that we really are applying God's principles. However, God has the only true definition of love. He has the only map that leads to real love. When we employ our own concepts of love, they fail to produce the desired results. Our methods, based on the world's system, promise love but actually remove it from our grasp. Because we call it love, we think it is the same thing that God's Word is describing. And though it may have a few similarities, if it does not match God's definition of love, it is not love. In the end we believe that God and people have failed us. Like a vaccination, it gives us just enough of the real thing so that we can't catch it.

> The most important thing in life is knowing and feeling love. This, of course, starts with God's

You Can Experience a Life of Love

When people live in a real loving relationship, they have something intangible but undeniable. They live in a realm that is sometimes euphoric. It is a place of safety and surety that pervades every other area of their lives. They have a secret strength. They appear to be safe when others are insecure. They seem impervious to much of the pain around them. They are experiencing the second half of Proverbs 13:12: *"But when the desire comes, it is a tree of life"* (NKJV). They have had their deepest desires fulfilled, and they are eating from the tree of life.

When Brenda and I got married, my life was pretty much a disaster. I was backslidden. I was very sick and faced the possibility of premature death. I was under incredible financial pressure. Yet I can remember looking her in the eyes and saying, "If we have love, if our home is a refuge of happiness, I can conquer the world." That was my simple plan for success: Find true fulfillment in a relationship and live out of that strength. Today, after more than twenty years of working that plan, my wife and I are living the dream life. The love in our home has brought healing to our children. It is a testimony to all who know us. It is the solace for all the pain of the past. It satisfies my soul.

Few people have an abiding sense of happiness. After thirty years of counseling and ministering to people, I would say that abiding, day-to-day happiness is unknown to most. But it doesn't have to be. The incredible thing about seeking a life of love is the way it affects everything. You can't grow in real love for your mate without growing in your love for God. Likewise, if you grow in your love for God, you will grow in your capacity to love other people.

Those who have spent their lives seeking the substitutes find life growing bitter and more disappointing with age. On the other hand, those who have the satisfaction of love—love for God and love for people—enjoy every new stage of life. Life becomes sweeter and more satisfying as the years go by.

The most important thing in life is knowing and feeling love. This, of course, starts with God's love. Why? Love is the basis of self-worth. It is the seat of every positive human emotion, while fear is the seat of every negative emotion. Apart from the experience of love, man cannot function as he was created to live.

Love, after all, is the goal of any meaningful relationship. People want to feel valued; they want to be precious to someone; they want to be special. We all want someone in our lives with whom we can connect. We want the emotions and actions that make us feel loved. Anything less, and pain is inevitable. However, wanting a wife is not the same as seeking a loving relationship. Finding a significant other does not necessarily cure loneliness. Great sex does not equate to a great relationship. In order for the goal of love to be accomplished, there must be an emotional connection expressed in a meaningful relationship. The apostle Paul said that love from a pure heart was the goal of all instruction. (See 1 Timothy 1:5.) John said, *"God is love"* (1 John 4:8).

> Love is a quality, a commitment, an experience, and actions—which combine to create a realm that is beyond what words can describe.

Love, although it must be experienced, is not just a feeling. Love is a quality, a commitment, an experience, and an action—all of which combine together to create a realm of existence that is beyond what mere words can describe. As I sit and consider the incredible love I have for my wife, I can't imagine any words to explain it. I feel her when I look into her eyes. I experience something when we hold hands. And this is from a guy who was never emotional or "touchy-feely"!

For centuries, great minds the world over—philosophers, poets, songwriters, and preachers—have sought to explain love in words that could be intellectually grasped, but to no avail. The total impossibility to verbally and intellectually express love brings me to the ultimate conclusion that it can be grasped only by those who have experienced it. And it can be experienced only by those who make it their individual life's purpose. Living in love—giving and receiving love in relationships with God and with people—is life's most important goal.

If we are to experience life at its best, we must put first things first. Before you read another chapter, you must decide the degree to which you will commit your life to walking in love. One night about twenty years ago, I determined that I wanted to know God's love and that I wanted to make the people around me feel loved. Next to my decision to accept Jesus as my Lord and Savior, this has been the most important commitment of my life. So make the decision and open the door to a life you have never known. Determine to pursue love today: Write your commitment in the flyleaf of your Bible and date it; put it on index cards on the mirror, the refrigerator, or any place that will stir your memory throughout the day! After you make this decision, the upcoming chapters will give you the tools you need to walk it out. But it starts with a decision today!

Chapter 4

What's Love Got to Do with It?

Chapter 4

What's Love Got to Do with It?

nlike the words to a hit song by Tina Turner imply, love has everything to do with everything! The bottom line for everything is God, and God is love. In fact, love and truth define God's character. *"God is love, and he who abides in love abides in God, and God in him"* (1 John 4:16 NKJV). Truth is no longer true if it is not applied in love. *"Love does no harm to a neighbor; therefore love is the fulfillment of the law"* (Romans 13:10 NKJV). Love is such an integral part of the Gospel that we are told to even love our enemies. (See Matthew 5:44.)

There is no understanding God unless we grasp His love.

> *Being rooted and grounded in love, may be able to comprehend with all the saints what is the width and length and depth and height; to know the love of Christ which passes knowledge; that you may be filled with all the fullness of God.* (Ephesians 3:17–19 NKJV)

The truth is, we can't even know God if we do not walk in love. *"He who does not love does not know God, for God is love"* (1 John 4:8 NKJV).

Bringing God into our marriage is not about following rules and fulfilling stereotypical roles; it is about bringing love into the relationship. Anything that God's Word advises for healthy husband-wife relationships turns into something negative and destructive if love is not the motivation and the goal. A godly relationship is a loving relationship!

But We Don't Want To...

How is it that we have missed this part of the Gospel? Simple! In our fear and unbelief, we really do not believe that love is God's nature. We do not believe He relates to us in love. And we do not believe that love will actually accomplish what we desire. We are like the man who asked Jesus what was required to inherit eternal life. Like many of us, the man knew the answer before he asked. He acknowledged that he should love God with all his being and love his neighbor as himself. That was a simple truth that anyone could understand. But there was someone he didn't want to love. Thus, his confusion was born out of his unwillingness to love someone whom he deemed unworthy. His intent is revealed in the next verse: *"But he, willing to justify himself, said unto Jesus, And who is my neighbour?"* (Luke 10:29).

There are always people we don't want to love and reasons we should not give our love to them. We can always find enough faults in others to justify our unwillingness. Naturally, we can use this against more people than just our spouses! Excuses, however, do not bring peace. No matter how we justify our unwillingness to love, in the end we are the ones who lose. We are the ones who spend our lives in lack and loneliness. We're alone, but we have an excuse! Nevertheless, excuses for not loving do not fill the emotional gaps.

The truth is, it is essential that we love our spouses, our children, our parents, and all others with unconditional love. Why? Because we are created in the likeness and image of God. Any attempt to live any other way defiles our spiritual, emotional, and physical existence. God is love, and we were created in His likeness. Deep beneath our façade of emotional protection is an incredible need to love as God loves.

God becomes understandable, as much as is possible, when we commit to walk in love.

Whether a person believes in God or not, he or she was created to be a loving being. Love is the root of our emotional and spiritual being. When we experience the new birth, through faith in Jesus, this need is intensified. Thus, we will never find our God-given destiny in friendship, business, or marriage until we love as He loves.

Make the Commitment

Starting this journey of love will require the most important, life-consuming decision you have ever made. You see, the love walk is a journey that requires every part of our lives. It usually starts in a specific area and slowly takes over our entire lives. In reality, it is the only way to actually walk with God. All else is religion and lip service. The way of love is the way of God. In marriage, all that is not love is not of God!

In thirty years of counseling I have encountered few situations that could not have been solved by a commitment to walk in love. Until that commitment is made, though, all else is just a religious substitute. I recall counseling a couple on the verge of divorce. The wife simply wanted the husband to meet a few very basic needs. To him, the needs seemed superficial. He chose to put his attention on what he considered to be her more important needs. Because he did not have enough value for his wife's needs, the marriage ended in divorce. He was totally surprised and completely devastated by the breakup. The truth was, he did not have enough love for his wife to do a few simple things that were important to her.

God becomes understandable, as much as is possible, when we commit to walk in love. Relationships become understandable only when we choose to walk in love. This is when the Gospel really makes sense in this chaotic world. It is in this commitment to walk in love that we are filled with the fullness and power of God.

> *To know the love of Christ which passes knowledge; that you may be filled with all the fullness of God. Now to Him who is able to do exceedingly abundantly above all that we ask or think, according to the power that works in us.*
> (Ephesians 3:19–20 NKJV)

When I talk about walking in love, I am not talking about becoming a doormat. I am not talking about the sick codependent tendencies that bring pain and suffering. Jesus walked in love, and He was never used. No one could ever take advantage of Him. If you have a fear of being used, please realize that nothing like that is part of walking in true love! Keep reading! Walking in God's love will empower you beyond anything you have ever known. It is the only protection from being used. Love for others emerges from a love for God and from a proper sense of God's love for me. If I have a sense of love, my dignity and self-worth will not allow me to be used or to live in degradation.

At this point you must begin to make some decisions, if you haven't already. Don't delay. Are you willing to make a commitment to walk in God's love? Will you make it your highest goal? You may know you are not able to do this in yourself, but the key is, "Are you willing?" If you are willing, then God can take you to this incredible place. Before you read any further, pray. Be honest with God. Tell Him where you stand regarding this issue. If you are not willing at this point, are you willing to have Him bring you to the place of willingness? God will start wherever you are willing to start. Admit your fears and concerns, but take the leap.

Please keep in mind that an unwillingness to commit to a life of love, by default, is a decision to spend the rest of your life in the outer circles of God's reality. You will always be near but never truly know. You will hear but never clearly see. You will smell but never taste. Your relationships with God and others will lack. Apart from a commitment to God's kind of love, you'll never find true abiding peace. Nothing else will satisfy. This is the pathway to all that you really need and desire in life. Choose love. You will see immediate changes in every area as you begin this journey!

Chapter 5

You Can't Give What You Don't Have

You Can't Give What You Don't Have

When most people come for marriage counseling, they think they will find rules or formulas that will make their marriage better. However, just knowing the right steps will not help people if they are not empowered to take those steps. It is like giving a couple a map, but no gasoline. Their frustration may increase; although they know where to go, they can't go without the "internal fuel." In other words, you can't give what you don't have.

Most of us know that we can't really walk in sacrificial love, especially toward those who are somehow unacceptable to us. But don't be discouraged by that; if you've recognized that fact, then you're in a great place! It can be the starting place of a new life! However, the problem is when, after recognizing our inability to full love, we try to justify it. Paul had a different perspective. He said, *"That is why, for Christ's sake, I delight in weaknesses, in insults, in hardships, in persecutions, in difficulties. For when I am weak, then I am strong"* (2 Corinthians 12:10 NIV).

In this Scripture passage Paul was talking about his experience with God's grace. He learned to feel safe when he faced what he could not do in his own strength. In other words, when he refused to depend on his own limited strength, he was able to experience God's unlimited strength. That is grace! Grace is God's ability, strength, and capacity that work from our hearts. It makes us able to do what we cannot do in our own strength.[2] Grace is God's ability that works through us when we know we can't do what is required. This principle is one of the cornerstones of all New Testament truth. Apart from God's grace, we all would be limited to doing as well as we could. Sometimes that is just not enough!

> Grace is God's ability, strength, and capacity working from our hearts. It makes us able to do what we cannot do in our own strength.

Religion tells you to love one another but doesn't give you anything to make it happen. Formulas tell us to be kind and patient. But if we don't feel kind and patient, our kindness and patience won't last very long. Love tells us to love our spouses. That sometimes seems impossible in the face of their actions. God, on the other hand, says, "I am going to give you the power to do it because I know you can't do what it takes in your own power."[3]

However, we can never experience grace as long as we say, "I can't!" Every time we face the realization of weakness, inability, or lack, we should *"come boldly unto the throne of grace, that we may obtain mercy, and find grace to help in time of need"* (Hebrews 4:16). God is always ready to give us the

[2] For a more in-depth study on grace, read *Grace: The Power to Change* (New Kensington, Pennsylvania: Whitaker House, 1993, 2001).

[3] John 1:16–17 says, *"And of His fullness we have all received, and grace for grace. For the law was given through Moses, but grace and truth came through Jesus Christ"* (NKJV).

help we need. He is our *"ever-present help in trouble"* (Psalm 46:1 NIV). I know I can't always walk in love if it depends on me. But I am sure I can walk in love if I want to, believe that through Christ I can, and make a decision to do so. I can be kind if I want to. God will give me the power. I can be patient when I choose to—and it is a choice. God gives us the power of choice. When we make choices that are consistent with His principles, we experience His power to see that decision through.

Changing Anger to Peace

I was a very angry person for about thirty years. I grew up with an innate sense of hatred. My earliest emotion, that I can remember, was hatred. I wanted to kill my father for his abuse to my mother. As you no doubt can guess, my deep-rooted anger led me to a life filled with conflict. By the time I gave my life to God, at age twenty-one, I was filled with rage. And although there was a major change in my life at salvation, I still had to deal with a quick temper and harshness. I was never influenced to make a commitment to walk in love as a new believer. It was never emphasized as a high priority in my early years as a Christian. Rather, love was something that was talked about only in a mystical sense. God loved us, but it seemed He also would hurt us and do cruel things. It was all so contradictory.

In time I began to see that I had good motives but a bad effect on many people. I wasn't someone who made you feel safe. Although I didn't give in to my anger very often, it was an obvious force that lurked just beneath the emotional surface. Even though I didn't express it, everyone could see it was there. The tone of voice, the raised eyebrow, the facial expression—all expressed something that I was not saying but was always feeling.

I was managing my anger, but I was not transforming into a peacemaker. Even when I did all the right things, there was seldom peace. My family loved me, but they were afraid of me. They always feared that what lay beneath the thin layer of self-control would emerge. It made people reluctant to challenge me. People walked on eggshells in my presence. It is emotionally tiring to always put forth effort to control negative emotions and actions. For many people, though, that is as close to victory as they will ever come. Perhaps this describes you. The continual internal struggles and repeated failures eventually convince you that you can't really overcome your problems and walk in love.

"I can't," however, is very often an excuse for "I don't want to." Our warped concepts of love make us think it entails weakness, frailty, losing control, giving up, or being a doormat. We have so conditioned ourselves to accept the world's definitions and ways of thinking that we do not believe we can get what we want from life and still walk in God's love. The two seem incompatible to the carnal mind. We even get angry just thinking that we have to love someone who has wronged us. It would seem we are doing them a favor! We feel foolish and used.

We only feel that way when we look at love through a heart that has been deceived by these corrupt philosophies. Love doesn't weaken; it empowers. It is the secret to faith and power. It is the seat of self-worth. We can never feel weak or defeated while walking in love. It provides clarity of perception. It opens us to all of God's possibilities in every situation.

Romans 12:2 says that I can experience transformation only to the degree that I renew my mind. In other words,

I have to see things the ways God spells them out in His Word before I can experience His transforming power. If I hold on to my old paradigms of life, love, and relationships, my relationships will never become any more than they have been. But as I accept God's perspective, as I accept His reality, I become empowered to live that reality.

Eventually I came to realize that walking in love brings me more benefit than it does anyone else.[4] Even if my wife doesn't appreciate it when I show love, even if she doesn't respond properly, it is an act of kindness to *myself.* I feel better about me, independent of her acceptance or response. Walking in love empowers me to be who I want to be regardless of who she is. It works the same way for her. As a result, we have freed ourselves from a reactionary relationship by walking in love.

The grace of God gives me the capacity to give and receive love.

I also believe, according to the Scriptures, that love never ceases to be effective. If love doesn't work, nothing will work. If love doesn't bring the response I desire, neither will anger or manipulation. So why bother wasting my time on another approach? And it did take time. I had to renew my mind about love—about what it is and how it works. I had to learn God's definition of love. I had to see that walking in love was the way to "win." I had to see love as a place of power instead of a place of vulnerability.

You Must Believe in Order to Experience

We can't, however, give what we do not have. We know what we have (or don't have) by what we are presently

---

[4] For more on this issue, read *How to Stop the Pain* (New Kensington, Pennsylvania: Whitaker House, 2001).

experiencing in our emotions. How does this work? First John 4:7–8 says, *"Beloved, let us love one another, for love is of God; and everyone who loves is born of God and knows God. He who does not love does not know God, for God is love"* (NKJV). The word *know* in the original language has to do with experiencing. It does not mean we have never met God if we do not love. It means we are not experiencing God if we do not love.

If you are inwardly experiencing something that makes you critical and faultfinding, it is not God and it is not love. If you are experiencing God, you will experience emotions of being loved and accepted. When you are experiencing love, it is easy to give it to others. You are sharing with them from the overflow of your personal experience. The way you relate to the people around you is simply a reflection of what you are currently experiencing in your own heart.

Many born-again believers are not experiencing the love of God. Why? They know they are believers, so why don't they experience His great love? The apostle John said that we must believe (and feel) the love of God. (See 1 John 4:16.) Feeling or experiencing anything from God starts with believing. Only when you believe the truth about what Jesus did for you will you begin to experience God's love.[5] This experience is more than a theological position. It is an inner realization that is experienced in your entire being. It is so consuming that it guides your life and becomes the seat of all your emotions. However, if you do not believe God loves you, you will not experience His love.

Twenty years ago I made the decision to know God's love and to help others know God's love. This was not a

---

[5] To read more on this topic, check out *The Gospel of Peace* (New Kensington, Pennsylvania: Whitaker House, 2002).

casual passing thought. It was a life commitment. I began by reading every Scripture in the New Testament that talked about the love of God, in every translation I had. I spent time every day acknowledging His love in my prayer life. I meditated on the love of God. I persuaded my heart of the truth of God's love.[6] And I made it a point to show love to others.

Every morning I reviewed the list of the love traits listed in 1 Corinthians 13. I pondered on how I could show these traits to people in my life. I even visualized myself facing difficult situations with more patience. I saw myself being more flexible and adaptable.

You cannot give what you don't have, and you cannot receive what you will not give.

After I had conversations with people, especially if those discussions were challenging, I would ask those people if they felt comfortable with the way it was handled. I started taking an up-to-the-minute inventory of the effect I was having on people.

As a result, the grace of God gave me the capacity to give and receive love. Since that time, my life and the lives of those around me have not been the same. Love has become the constant motivation in my life. I wake up in the morning with an incredible sense of love and acceptance. I have peace in my heart. Even when I could justify anger, I feel an overwhelming desire and ability to walk in love. Compassion and patience flow very naturally. I look forward to making people feel loved.

I also discovered, after I made my decision to walk in love, that grace is a two-sided coin. In other words, you cannot give what you don't have, and you cannot receive

---

[6] For help in organizing your prayer life, I recommend *The Prayer Organizer* (Huntsville, Alabama: Impact International Publications, 1985).

what you will not give. If you attempt to give love without believing the truth about God's love, it will be a vain, short-lived effort. If you seek to feel God's love with no commitment to love others, you will never be empowered. It will be a never-ending search. The apostle John said it like this: *"If we love one another, God dwelleth in us, and his love is perfected in us"* (1 John 4:12). The Living Bible says it even more clearly: *"When we love each other God lives in us, and his love within us grows ever stronger."*

Besides the personal, internal benefits of walking in love, my marriage has become a haven of peace. My wife and my children feel safe talking to me. I have helped create an environment where it is safe for us all to walk in love and openness. Peace, friendship, and fun have become the experience in our household.

Do you want to wake up every morning with positive emotions of love and acceptance toward your spouse and everyone else around you? How do you think your marriage, family relationships, and world around you would change if every moment of every day you felt God's love? Would you be happier if you could feel the love of your spouse, children, and friends? All of this and more is within your reach. But, it starts with a decision. In the previous chapter you made a decision to know God's love. In this chapter I am asking you to make a commitment to *give* love. Before you read on, pray and tell God where you are and what you are feeling. Tell Him your fears and concerns. Own your stuff! Yet, in the end, let Him know that the life of love is the life you intend to live. When you do, His grace will come more alive in you with every step you take!

Chapter 6

Awakening God's Love in Our Hearts

Awakening God's Love in Our Hearts

To understand love more clearly, let's look at it from God's perspective. In 1 John, the Scriptures say that God is love. In Greek this word is *agape*. In English we only have one word for love, but Greek has four different words. Each one describes a different aspect and quality of love. Now, this unique kind of love mentioned in 1 John is not simply something God does when He is in a certain mood; neither is it something He experiences when we have done enough to appease Him. No, *agape*-love is who He is, and there is nothing we can do to change His character. So until we understand this love, any attempt at knowing God is little more than an adventure in our vain religious imaginations.

You may wonder what God's *agape*-love has to do with romantic love. This *agape* is the highest form of love and is the basis for all other healthy types of love. It will be from this quality of love that we are able to bring forth and sustain a passionate loving relationship. It is this very love that can keep a marriage passionate and romantic for a lifetime. It is this love that every person needs and seeks. When we yield to God's *agape*-love in us, it becomes a consuming way of life that breeds every aspect of love.

Agape-Love Is...

Let's look at this a little more closely. *Agape*-love can and should have feelings, yet it supercedes mere emotion. It is the defining aspect of our character. It emerges from the very seat of our nature. It forges our identity. It is actions that materialize from intent. It looks for the opportunity to do good to another. It is self-sacrificial, yet it never loses self. It will lay down its life for another, but it will never do another's part. It will empower to godliness but never enable base code-pendent tendencies. It is a merging of truth and mercy. It always reflects God's life-giving nature. It is effective when all else fails.

Agape is the highest form of love and can keep a marriage passionate and romantic for a lifetime.

Paul best described the attributes of love in the familiar passage of 1 Corinthians 13:4–7.

> *Love is patient, love is kind. It does not envy, it does not boast, it is not proud. It is not rude, it is not self-seeking, it is not easily angered, it keeps no record of wrongs. Love does not delight in evil but rejoices with the truth. It always protects, always trusts, always hopes, always perseveres.* (NIV)

These are all actions—actions that are based in the character of God. This is how God relates to us. This is how we should relate to one another.

Kenneth S. Wuest eloquently describes God's *agape*-love. "It is a love called out of a person's heart by 'an awakened sense of value in an object which causes one to prize it.' It expresses a love of approbation and esteem. It is a love that recognizes the worthiness of the object loved."[7] Approbation is synonymous with approval and admiration. This takes on an entirely unique perspective when we realize that John 3:16 could be interpreted to say, "For God had such value, approval, and admiration for the world that He gave His only begotten Son...." It is amazing to think that this is the quality of love God has for mankind.

In Matthew 5:43–48, Jesus said that we should be children who are like our Father. We should have hearts that are willing to love our enemies, bless those who curse us, and pray for those who spitefully use us. We should have the love that causes us to do good to the deserving and undeserving. He wants this because this is who He is and how He functions. This is the only thing that will bring wholeness and happiness to an individual and to a relationship. For instance, there have been days when Brenda and I loved one another as friends, and then there were days we loved each other even though we felt like enemies.

It is this agape-love that can keep a marriage passionate and romantic for a lifetime.

Love for Love's Sake, Not Your Sake

All the actions love takes are for the other person's well-being. They are not for our benefit, although they do benefit us. Love does not have a humanistic agenda. The goal of all love's actions is to help people experience God through us. All our love's actions are designed to point people to a loving God who can, in fact, meet their every need. And although this love meets the needs of the other

---

[7] Kenneth S. Wuest, *Word Studies in the Greek New Testament*, Vol. III (Grand Rapids, Michigan: Wm B. Eerdmans Publishing Company, 1968), 112.

person, it is this very love that causes others to open up to us. It causes people to respond to us in an incredibly positive manner.

After a long, tiring day, I came home and found that Brenda wanted to go for a bicycle ride. She said, "I know you don't really want to go riding and I am willing to go by myself, but I would enjoy it a lot more if you went." I really didn't want to go. I was tired and would have preferred to rest. But, I agreed. "All right, I'll change clothes and we'll ride." When I stood up to go change, she put her arms around me, gave me a long, sweet kiss and said, "I really do love you." A simple act of kindness prompted several days of passion and affection.

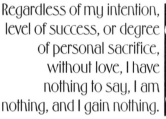

Regardless of my intention, level of success, or degree of personal sacrifice, without love, I have nothing to say, I am nothing, and I gain nothing.

In the first three verses of 1 Corinthians 13, Paul pointed out that all our actions are meaningless if they are not motivated by love.

> *If I speak in the tongues of men and of angels, but have not love, I am only a resounding gong or a clanging cymbal. If I have the gift of prophecy and can fathom all mysteries and all knowledge, and if I have a faith that can move mountains, but have not love, I am nothing. If I give all I possess to the poor and surrender my body to the flames, but have not love, I gain nothing.* (NIV)

Regardless of my intention, regardless of my levels of worldly success, regardless of the degree of my personal sacrifice, without love I have nothing to say, I am nothing, and I gain nothing. According to God's Word, the only pathway to have and experience all that life has to offer is to walk in love.

Unfortunately, many of these positive actions are done for the wrong reason. Kindness for the hope of personal gain is not kindness; it is manipulation. Too often we perform these things for our benefit. We use them as payments toward a desired response. It is then that our motives are questioned. More than once when I have done something kind for Brenda, she would respond, "That would mean a lot more if I didn't know that you want something."

One of the most frequent lines spouses give while in marriage counseling is, "Just tell me what you want me to do, and I'll do it." As noble as that sounds, it is rarely met with trust or appreciation. To the one who has been neglected, it sounds like the other is saying, "I'll do what you want if it will get me what I want."

When we pay attention, it says, "I have value for you!" When we make the other person feel valued, it stirs passion and romance.

Neglected individuals want you to do what you do because you have value for their feelings. Your spouse wants to know that you pay attention to him or her, notice what he or she likes, notice what brings him or her joy. There are men who know the statistics of every player in the NFL but don't have a clue what their wives' favorite colors are. The truth is, we put our attention on the things we value. When we don't know what our spouses enjoy, we aren't paying attention.

If you wait until a crisis comes to ask what your mate wants you to do, the answer you're going to hear is, "If I have to tell you, it won't mean anything when you do it."

We *can* awaken God's love in us. It all starts when we allow ourselves to experience God's love. It enters our marriage when we make the commitment to give that love to our spouses and families. Then we start noticing, communicating, and paying attention! When we pay attention, it says, "I have value for you!" When we remember what is important to our spouses or what they like, it says, "I have value for you." When we do the things that make the other person feel valued, it stirs a passion and romance that is beyond our imagination!

Over the next few days start doing a little "undercover" work. Without your mate knowing it, start discovering things about him or her. Find out his or her likes and dislikes. Look for what brings your spouse pleasure and worth. Then surprise him or her by doing some of those things. When you do them, however, do not expect a sexual response. Just do them. Follow this process for all of the people who are important in your life. Learn to notice what people value. Let them discover the joy of love that comes because you notice. It will awaken love in both your heart and theirs!

Chapter 7

Love Responses

Chapter 7

Love Responses

We all want our mates to give us a life of passion and romance. We want our spouses to light our emotional flame. We want to know what it is like to be stirred deep within our beings. We want to be loved freely and completely. The problem is, however, we want our *mates* to give us this type of love. We want them to initiate it. We want our spouses to make us feel it. We want the other person to do for us what we can do only for ourselves.

Remember, the *agape*-love of God is something that emerges from our relationship with God. It is our response to His love and value for us. But the kind of love that emerges because people like us and have passion for us is their response to us. There is a Greek word for natural affection, but it seems to have hints of obligation. It does not arise from deep passion. It is not a response to our love. It is more instinctive. That is certainly not what we are looking for in marriage!

The Bible speaks of a love that is found in friendship, affection or fondness. It comes from the Greek word *phileo*. While the *agape*-love concerns an issue of value, *phileo* is a response to what appeals to us as pleasurable.[8] People give this kind of love to someone whom they perceive as creating pleasure for them. In other words, people will not respond to you in friendship, fondness, or affection if they do not view their involvement with you as pleasurable.

We seem to understand that when we are dating we have to be pleasurable. We know that if our dates do not have a good time, they will not go out with us again. Yet after marriage, it seems we assume we have some new right to evoke obligation. We no longer put forth the same effort to be pleasurable, and therefore the way our mates respond to us changes. The solution to changing the response is to change our stimuli. Instead of looking to  our spouses when they are not warm and affectionate, we should look to us. The seed (input) determines the crop (response). God calls that the law of sowing and reaping.

Do I make you feel special? Do you feel safe with me? Do I make you feel good about yourself?

When we walk in *agape*-love by demonstrating great value for people, they usually perceive us to be individuals who bring pleasure to their lives. By being sensitive, caring, and attentive to their needs, we evoke a passionate response in the people we love. As we respond to God's love by expressing value to the people around us, they in turn respond to us with affection. If the people we love are not giving us affection, we must question the quality of *agape*-love we are giving them. All the while we must remember that giving *agape*-love is not a manipulation game to get a certain response, even though we know that nothing else will give us the response we desire.

---

[8] Kenneth S. Wuest, *Word Studies in the Greek New Testament*, Vol. III (Grand Rapids, Michigan: Wm. B. Eerdmans Publishing Company, 1968), 109.

One of the best ways to measure our effectiveness at showing love is to simply ask questions. Here are a few good ones to ask your mate: "Do I make you feel special? Do you feel safe with me? Do I make you feel good about yourself? Is there anything I expect of you that violates your sense of dignity?" There are hundreds of important questions that need to be asked on a regular basis. And though we might not like the answers, those answers hold the key to our romantic future.

Love without Motivation

Too often people think they can demand someone's affection. Save your energy! Demanding affection is like trying to put toothpaste back in the tube. It is a journey in control that results in the loss of trust, love, and passion. You cannot demand that people be fond of you. You can't demand them to desire your company. You can't even require them to sit in the same room with you. You may force external compliance, but you will never get a passionate response. You can, however, treat people in such a way that their involvement with you is a pleasurable experience that stirs the flames of passionate love. After all, wouldn't you want your spouse to look forward to being with you, rather than feeling obligated?

There is a reason passionate love is called desire. Obligation is not desire. We will never connect with the person who responds out of fear, obligation, desperation, or control. We may get some of our physical needs met, but our longing for intimacy will never be fulfilled. Obligation can get physical involvement but not romantic passion. It can get sex but not intimacy. And sex without intimacy is the breeding ground for sexual abuse.

The heart that has been corrupted by the world's view of love and sex—the Hollywood version—thinks that the craving for intimacy is a craving for sex. These people force themselves on their mates. They use guilt, obligation, and a host of other fear-based tactics. They make a person cooperate, but they will never make that person desire them.

The apostle John said, *"Beloved, if God so loved us, we ought also to love one another"* (1 John 4:11). God never demands us to love Him. As a matter of fact, the Scriptures say that *"we love him, because he first loved us"* (1 John 4:19). He doesn't demand our love. He loves us until we respond. It is His goodness that draws us to repentance, not His demands. (See Romans 2:4.) If we give *agape*-love to a person who is capable of experiencing love, he or she will respond to us in an affectionate manner. The question is, are we willing to *agape*-love a person until he or she is able to respond in a healthy manner?

> People who love have value for the other person's feelings and want every interaction to be positive, enjoyable, and emotionally compelling.

This is, of course, such a paradox. Selfish people don't care if the other person enjoys their company, their affection, or their sex life. They just want to use their mates for personal gratification. The unspoken message is, "I don't have value for you. I do not hold esteem for you." In short, they say, "I don't really love you. I just want to use you for my gratification." Such a person may even be willing to give a form of conditional love: "I'll treat you nice and do good things for you if I get what I want. But if you don't give me what I want, I will pout or do petty things to punish you."

People who love have value for the other person's feelings and want every interaction to be positive, enjoyable, and emotionally compelling. They want the other person to have desire for them. They will be as patient and strategic as need be. Although the benefits that emerge from giving *agape*-love are a real probability, walking in *agape*-love is about far more than that. *Agape* finds joy in the fulfillment that the other person experiences from their efforts. The great enjoyment comes from knowing that the person they value benefits so much from their love.

> If the people we love are not giving us affection, we must question the quality of love we are giving them.

So many times when Brenda was kind and patient with me, I did not initially respond properly. But her persistent patience usually reached my heart and stirred something within me. It compelled me to desire her. It compelled me to treat her with more respect. The fact that she has often treated me far better than I deserve has led to personal healing for me and has been an incredible strength in our marriage.

Sexual Passion Still Requires Agape

As I mentioned in a previous chapter, there is yet another Greek word for love, which is *eros*. It is the word from which we get the English word *erotic*. According to Wuest, "It is a passion seeking satisfaction."[9] It is a seeking of satisfaction that seizes the whole mind. Erotic love is a love that comes from passion. Erotic love, like affection, is a response. It is a response that we should learn to evoke in our mates. A person who does not take the time to facilitate a passionate response before sexual intimacy will never satisfy his or her mate.

On the other hand, eroticism without *agape*-love destroys dignity and self-worth. Eroticism alone says, "Can you

---

[9] Ibid.

satisfy my craving? I want to use you for satisfaction." The other person then has value only as a sexual object. But when *agape*-love is the stimulus for erotic love, value has already been established. Dignity remains intact. Sexual intimacy then fulfills the more God-given role of creating a bond and connection through mutual satisfaction.

For true erotic love to emerge requires great trust. Many people fear the vulnerability of erotic love. They fear allowing another person to have access to these types of deep emotions. Nevertheless, when people feel so valued, so held in esteem, and so safe, they will allow themselves to share the vulnerability of erotic passion. If our mates do not feel valued and safe, we will never touch the depths of their desire, which longs to express their love through their entire beings.

Make your mate feel safe, valued, and special. Never ask him or her to participate in what would diminish self-worth. That makes the bedroom a place of degradation and humiliation. Intimacy becomes a dread instead of a delight. Never rush to self-gratification. Take the time necessary to evoke the responses that both you and your mate desire. If you walk in *agape*, your mate's response will be from his or her whole being. When you allow a person the freedom of response, you get his or her whole heart!

Because Brenda had a background of sexual and physical abuse, she had a lot of very conflicting emotions about lovemaking. She desired me, but she had all these negative associations. Because I have always sought to make our lovemaking something special, exciting, and intimate, we have grown together in these areas beyond what either of us ever believed possible. More than once after we have made love and I am holding her in my arms, she has said, "I never believed that I would ever want to make love with someone as much as I want you."

How does your mate feel about him or herself after lovemaking? Do you find yourself seeking personal gratification to the extent that you are willing to violate your partner's sense of dignity? Talk to your spouse. Find out how your spouse feels. Make a commitment to never pressure or ask for anything that your mate finds unpleasant or unfulfilling. Give your spouse the freedom to lose him or herself in passionate love as he or she responds to your *agape*.

Chapter 8

Your Pearl of Great Price

Chapter 8

Your Pearl of Great Price

One day you stood before your mate and you made a vow. Hopefully you made it from your heart. It was a vow to "love, honor, and cherish, keep in sickness and in health, and to forsake all others and keep yourself unto her (or him) for as long as you both shall live." This is a vow to give *agape*-love! You made those vows because at that moment your new mate was your "pearl of great price."

Jesus gave this parable about value, the parable of the pearl of great price: *"Again, the kingdom of heaven is like a merchant seeking beautiful pearls, who, when he had found one pearl of great price, went and sold all that he had and bought it"* (Matthew 13:45–46 NKJV). There is a principle in this parable that says when we find something of value, we will sell all else to obtain that valuable object. Although this parable applies this principle to the kingdom of God, the principle actually applies to every area of life. And there is no arena where it is more applicable than marriage!

When we first found our mates, they were our pearls of great price. We were willing to give up all our freedoms and risk our emotional and even our material well-being for the other person. We expressed our value for this person with all our hearts. Our bride or groom knew that we held him or her in this great value. That is why there is such a flood of affection and passion early in a relationship. All we see and express is how precious and valuable our new love is.

Then, when the "honeymoon phase" ends, things begin to change. The two people who were once so passionate and loving now hardly touch one another. There is little affection, and romance is a hope deferred! Now our hearts are sick. We feel we will never have what we once longed for with this person. We wonder where the love went. What happened to the passion?

True Passion Requires Value

I cannot count the number of people I have counseled who were passionate for their mates when they were dating or early in their marriage but who now despise their touch. Too many men, being driven purely by the need to satisfy their sexual passion, make their wives feel they are of value only when they meet their husbands' sexual needs. Driven by the self-centered, immature need for gratification, the man unwittingly sends that message. When men pressure for sex, pout when they don't get it, and expect sexual rewards for every act of kindness, they send a message that says, "I do not have *agape*-love for you. I do not value you as a person. I do not hold you in high esteem. You are not precious to me. You are only an object that I use for self-gratification."

Too often we begin our marriages with more personal passion than *agape*-love. Remember, eroticism apart from *agape* is self-centered. It becomes purely an act of self-gratification. In many cases we are young and inexperienced.

In other cases we are hurt from the past and influenced by previous fears and failures. Too many marriages have begun without the tools necessary to build the relationship that was hoped for.

The absence of communication skills, the presence of awkwardness—these factors cause us to enter sexual relations with no clue of how to develop love and sustain dignity. I once counseled a man who did everything he could to make himself sexually potent. He said, "I intend to ruin women for any other man." He took herbs; he learned sexual skills; and, physically, I guess he did it all. He thought these things would make women love him. But there has never yet been a woman who felt loved by him. The great sex wasn't enough to make anyone trust him or want to spend her life with him. He had passion, yes. But his passion did not emerge from great value and a meaningful relationship. His passion emerged from an ego need to be a sexual "stud-muffin." He is one of the loneliest men I know!

When a couple is first "in love," they have their pearl of great price. They have such incredible value for one another. Too often, though, that value is for the *benefits* the person brings instead of for the *person*. Too often the courtesy and kindness is little more than the drive for the reward of sexual intimacy, security, or some other self-seeking cause.

Erotic passion can wear a mask that looks very much like *agape*. It can be kind, patient, and thoughtful. But it is motivated by a passion that seeks gratification. Sometimes the passion is for sex; sometimes it is for safety; sometimes it is for the need to be loved. Nevertheless, if passion is not motivated by great value for the other person, it is not *agape*-love. It is not self-sacrificial; it is self-seeking. The Bible says,

"For where…self-seeking exist[s]*, confusion and every evil thing are there"* (James 3:16 NKJV).

The problem is, when erotic passion exists without *agape*, the pearl of great price is not so great after conquest. Or when self-gratification doesn't get everything it wants, it is not long until the kindness and compliments disappear. A new tactic emerges, and before long a couple sinks into the depths of inflicting pain on each other.

Whatever the reason, one day we start taking our pearl of great price for granted. We stop noticing and appreciating the things we value about our spouses. We start considering the things they do for us as an obligation instead of an act of kindness. To the degree we make them feel obligated, we receive back from them only what they feel is their obligation. When affection disappears, instead of looking at the way we treat them, we focus on how they are treating us. Rather than attempting to foster loving responses, we become more critical and demanding. We express less value and push them farther from us.

Appreciation and value are no longer expressed or felt. To the degree we perceive we have no value to our mates, to the degree we feel used or taken for granted, we stop responding. Affection and passion sink to the level of our sense of value. Sometimes we wish we could find that former passion and affection. Sometimes we condemn ourselves because we are not responding to them properly.

Brenda and I have learned to express appreciation for everything, no matter how often the person does it. Just because she has cooked thousands of meals for me does not mean she is obligated. I try always to let her know I appreciate every meal. She reminds me that she appreciates my patience with her in certain areas.

We both have been in enough bad relationships to know that we can't expect anything of anyone. Even when we don't do things just as the other would prefer, we still appreciate the effort.

Keep Your Pearl in Mind

Usually our mates are responding properly. It may not be the response we want, but it is the response our actions evoke. When we find ourselves being the one who is not responding well, we can take the opportunity to introduce *agape*-love into the emotional mix. We can choose to rise above the level of reactionary living and choose to show *agape*-love. We can be patient and kind because of who we are in Jesus. On the other hand, if our mates want affection (*phileo*) and passion (*eros*), they must bring that which evokes those responses. We should always give *agape*. The absence of passion and affection should be indicators that we are not planting the right seeds.

Agape is the only hope for your marriage. If that does not work, nothing will.

Regardless of which side of the coin you find yourself on, the key to changing everything is communication. When we don't feel we can be responsive to our mates, our job is to express how they make us feel.[10] Their job is to listen and respond.

Just the other day, Brenda approached me about a somewhat delicate issue. Unfortunately, she did not discuss this with me when it was small. She wasn't sure of how to approach it. As a result, it kind of stewed beneath the surface and came out at an inopportune time and in an unacceptable manner.

---

[10] For more on this topic, read *How to Stop the Pain* (New Kensington, Pennsylvania: Whitaker House, 2001).

This took place after we had had several weeks of incredible closeness and passion. Inwardly, I felt some of the old feelings of rejection attempt to rise up. The thought briefly emerged, *See, it doesn't do any good to try. Something always goes wrong.* Fortunately, I do not entertain those types of deceitful thoughts. Several weeks of happiness is worth it even if something does go wrong.

After Brenda had "vented" on me, she was all right with everything, but I wasn't. I was a little insulted. However, instead of carrying that offense around for weeks, I talked to her the next day. (It took me a day to determine how to best approach it and not create more problems.) I shared with her how her communication made me feel. I explained that I would be far more likely to deal with the issue if it is not complicated by hurt feelings. We talked about positive ways to communicate about these kind of issues. The problem was solved.

If we had not talked that thing through, I would have stopped being responsive to her romantic advances. My reaction would have brought about the end of several weeks of strong passion and affection. Instead, we picked up where we left off. The only difference was that we strengthened our communication and trust instead of damaging them.

In those moments of hurt, rejection, or frustration, we can easily forget all that we value about our mates. We can throw away the pearl of great price. We can damage it beyond repair. Early in our marriage when Brenda and I would fight, I would think, *I don't know why I married this woman. I can't think of one thing about her that I like.* Then when we recovered from the argument I would think, *I love everything about her. She is the perfect wife.* I have learned that when conflict or pain arises, I must remember what it is that is precious to me about her. I must remember all the reasons she is my pearl of great price.

In some marriages there really was a degree of genuine love in the beginning, but through self-centeredness or ignorance, it was not long before hurt and disappointment pushed the couple far from one another. When *agape* is not the motivating factor, it really doesn't matter what was present at the beginning of your marriage. You still reach the same emotional end as the user and abuser. You find yourself in the place of emptiness, loneliness, despair, and rejection. Looking back to judge the motive of your mate will not solve the problem. Deciding to bring *agape*-love into you relationship is the only cure.

Make a list of all of the things you have ever valued about your mate. Try to notice how many of them are still there but of which you have become unappreciative. If your spouse has stopped doing the things you value, ask why. Be ready for answers that you don't like. Do not defend yourself, and do not argue. Remind yourself to express appreciation for everything your mate does. Sometimes a simple "thank you" is enough. Sometimes a special response is in order. Even when the effort does not produce what you want, express appreciation for the effort. As Shania Twain says in her song, "Any Man of Mine," "When I cook him dinner, and I burn it black, he better say 'Mmmm, I like it like that!'"[11] Make your mate the pearl of great price once again and see what he or she makes you.

---

[11] Shania Twain and John "Mutt" Lange, "Any Man of Mine," performed by Shania Twain. Loon Echo Music, 1995. *The Woman in Me*. Compact disc.

Chapter 9

How's That Working for You?

Chapter 9

How's That Working for You?

Someone has said, "Practice does not make perfect; it just makes permanent!" Those things that we do become more concrete every time we do them, whether they are effective or ineffective. For me, one of the saddest sights in the world is seeing someone who is sincere but sincerely wrong. Why? This person keeps trying harder and harder at the wrong things. Sometimes it seems that such people are more desperate to be right than to be effective. Instead of asking what they could do that is more effective, they keep assuming they are right. With the need to be right driving their actions, they keep trying harder, sometimes making the problem worse. The problem is that their actions are based on assumptions!

With that thought in mind, what are you doing to initiate love in your relationship? Did these efforts arise from meaningful communication with your mate or from your assumptions? Did you ever ask the other person what he or she wanted? Have you asked how your efforts make your mate feel? So I'll ask you, "How's it working for you?" Is your life and marriage going where you want it to go? Are you seeing the desired results? Have you discovered the key to unlocking the doors of affection and passion? Or are you feeling frustrated and unappreciated?

Do You Want to Be Right or Happy?

Much of the hurt that we encounter comes from what we perceive to be a lack of appreciation. When people don't express appreciation for our efforts, we don't feel valued (*agape*). Then our responses to them become negative. This is often the beginning of a lifelong syndrome of effort, frustration, rejection, and pain. We must realize that a person may value us, but not value our efforts. Sometimes when we insist on showing love our way, it comes across to the other person as manipulation and insensitivity.

The truth is that your spouse does not value those efforts. I have counseled many angry couples. The feelings of disapproval in the face of their efforts drove them to outrage. Hundreds of times I have watched as one person said to the other, "That's not what I wanted." The other, blinded by anger, retorts, "I'm not going to do anything else for you if you don't appreciate what I've already done!" Why should our mates value our efforts? After all, we did not value their feelings enough to ask them what was important to them. We didn't ask them what would make them feel special and loved. We, in our arrogance, said, "This is what I want to do for you, so this should be enough!" It isn't! So my question is, "How's that working for you?" Do you want to keep doing what you've always done with the same frustrating results, or do you want to try something else?

Showing love our way can come across as manipulative and insensitive.

Sadly, more people would rather be right than be happy. One of the most common questions I ask when I am in marriage counseling is this: "What could your mate do to make you feel loved and cause you to want to stay?" The answers that I get are usually incredibly simple. I can't believe people are ready to divorce when the solution is so easily within their reach. So in that session I get an agreement from the person that says he or she wants to save the marriage. The person agrees to show love in a way that his or her mate values.

Usually, the couple comes back a week later to evaluate what has happened. It is rare that the person has done any of those things requested. When I ask, "Why didn't you do these things that would make your spouse feel loved?" the answers vary. Sometimes I hear, "Why should I have to do those things? What about him (or her)? What is she (or he) going to do?" The most common one, however, is, "That's stupid. Why does she want me to do that? It doesn't make any sense to me." "Why should I have to pick up my clothes? I have worked all day. Isn't that her job?" "Well," I ask, "how's that approach working for you? When you explained it that way, did it make her fall in love with you?"

I sat down with one of my children and her husband as they were working through some of these very issues. She had small children to tend to every day. She wanted him to pick up after himself more. She explained her need for help raising two small children. She said, "I have never seen my mom pick up after my dad. When he takes his clothes off he puts them in the clothes basket. When he gets out of the tub, he puts the towel and washcloth where they go."

He asked me, "Don't you think that is Brenda's job, especially since she doesn't work outside of the home?" I said, "Sure it's her job. But we had five kids and a big house. Every time I picked up after myself, it was a help to her. Now that our kids are grown and she has less to do, she especially appreciates it. It is an act of love."

The "fly in the ointment" has been revealed when one of the partners just wants to do what makes sense to him or her. In such cases, these people want love on their terms, by their definition, not God's. They want what they consider to be fair, something that God never considers in His love for us. Such people would rather be right than sacrifice, step beyond the comfort zone, and do what someone else values. They would rather be right than happy. *Agape*-love, however, is always motivated by what brings value and esteem to the other person.

> Love is always motivated by what brings value and esteem to the other person.

Again my question, "How's that working for you?" Is your stubborn resistance getting you what you want? No? Then why keep trying what has never worked and will never work?

Do What Works

Love (*agape*) values the person. Likewise, if I really value you as a person, I will value what you value. I will value what brings you happiness and esteem. It doesn't have to make sense to me. Because of the positive way it affects you, I will gain value for what you value. My value for you causes me to see things in a new light.

My wife loves jewelry. I don't like jewelry. It makes no sense to me. You can buy cubic zirconium that looks real for a lot less. So why waste your money? My wife, on the other hand, can spot a fake diamond in a heartbeat. I tried to convince her of my logic, but she didn't buy it.

Early in our marriage, when we were incredibly broke, I didn't have the money to buy her nice jewelry, and she didn't pressure me. She knew we did not have the money.

She appreciated my effort when I would buy her flowers and a card, but that wasn't of much value to her.

At first I felt great despair. I felt pressured. I projected a pressure on myself that she wasn't creating. Instead, *I* was creating it from my feelings of failure as a husband and provider. The Bible says that faith works by love. (See Galatians 5:6.) I loved my wife, and I knew God loved me. For me, this meant there was a way, but I wasn't seeing it. Self-pity tempted me to fret and find fault with her to justify my money issues.

I didn't want to live in self-pity, though. I wanted my wife to have the things that brought her pleasure and fulfillment. One day when a particular special occasion was coming up, I took her to a very nice jewelry store. We looked at all the nice jewelry. I wanted so badly to buy something for her, but I did not have the money or the credit.

After window-shopping for a while, she was ready to go. But I asked which piece she liked the most. She showed me. Then I asked her if she wanted me to buy it. She knew we could not afford it. Still, I gave her the options. "Would you rather I buy you something that I can afford now, or would you like for me to take the money I was going to spend and put this ring on layaway?"

That day we put a very nice ring on layaway. She was so happy. Every time I had a little extra money I paid on it, and in a few months we got it. She loved it! But as much as anything she loved the fact that I got past my hang-ups about jewelry and recognized the pleasure that it brought her.

For many years I bought nice jewelry on layaway. I am so thankful that today I am able to afford nice things for her. Yet I am glad I didn't wait until today to do those things. Most of all, I am glad I did not allow my personal hang-ups to prevent me from expressing love to my wife in a way that she appreciated.

Buying jewelry still doesn't make a lot of sense to me. Having a happy, responsive wife does make a lot of sense. Most of the jewelry I bought her was a special expression of my love for her. Every time she wears any of her jewelry, it stirs something in her that makes her feel very special. It expresses a love beyond words. It conveys the fact that I value her enough to hear and respect what she values.

One of the most unique things I have experienced from this type of love has been in the area of personal prosperity. I grew up with a poverty mentality. I felt guilty if I had anything nice. Success seemed like a pursuit of ego that served only to corrupt the heart. This thinking negatively affected every area of my life. My issues with money could have prevented me from finding ways to express my love for my wife and family.

Love, however, made me want to give a better life to my family. Love empowered me to face my issues with poverty and prosperity. I now had a reason to prosper beyond myself. As I was motivated to give my wife the best, I came to realize that God's love for me was far greater. He wanted me to have the best. I have to say this new thinking has worked very well for me. I've got a wife who loves and appreciates me, and I have been able to face a major obstacle that ran many generations deep in my family.

Faith works by love. Love for our mates can empower us to face issues that were previously hidden and justified. Love stretches us to believe God in new areas. There are few areas of my life that have not been stretched because of the love Brenda and I share. So I have to say, "This is working great for me!"

How are your efforts working for you? Do you do things that seem to be unappreciated? Have you asked your mate what he or she would enjoy? If it is beyond your reach, have you prayed and planned ways to make it attainable? Do you find that you are more interested in being right than having a peaceful, loving environment? If what you are doing isn't working, ask your spouse. Let him or her tell you what will work. Then trust God to empower you with His grace and stretch you beyond where you are.

Chapter 10

Touching the Heart

Chapter 10

Touching the Heart

I f you really want to connect with your mate, you will have to get beyond the mere outward observance of plans and strategies. "Connecting" is about touching the heart. I learned that I could never touch my wife's heart unless I was constantly aware, paying attention, and staying sensitive. The person who connects never assumes anything. Life is a dynamic exchange of information and emotions, of verbal and non-verbal communication that requires the highest level of attentiveness.

One of the wisest men who ever lived said, *"There is a time for everything, and a season for every activity under heaven"* (Ecclesiastes 3:1 NIV). Life is a constant ebb and flow of different seasons; it is continual change. The wise person recognizes the seasons and coordinates his or her efforts accordingly.

For instance, there is a time to plant the seed and a time to harvest the crop. A farmer's success is closely related to his ability to interpret what season he is in and to adjust his activities accordingly. It would not make sense to plant corn in the middle of winter. Such is every aspect of life, including relationships.

No matter how good your relationship was at any earlier time, this is today. Things were a certain way when you were dating. Then when you married, it all changed. Many marriages today are lost simply because people want it to be the way it was when they dated. I have news for you: It will never be the way it was! When you marry, you take on the new responsibilities of bills, schedules, and the amount of time spent together. There is a greater need for communication, sensitivity, and planning.

Then the children start popping in. Now the husband is no longer the focus of his wife's affection. She is physically exhausted from caring for a child, more specifically *their* child. Her emotions and physical health may change because of the extreme physical stress of having a baby. A great sex life is little more than memory for a while.

The self-centered person approaches these changes seeking to find some way to prevent the loss of previous benefits. This person's lack of understanding and unwillingness to adjust sends a message to his or her spouse that says, "I don't care about you. I just want to know if you will still meet my needs."

In nearly thirty years of marriage counseling, I have found that the two most common places where women come to despise their sex life is on the honeymoon and after the birth of the first child. In these times when a husband needs to be tender and understanding, he often becomes demanding and self-seeking. Sex becomes a major issue with little concern for the emotional or physical well-being of the wife. For many couples, their sex life takes a downhill turn at these vulnerable junctures and never recovers. What was once sacred and sweet becomes crude and harsh.

At every change in life, needs and expectations of both partners change. It is the mark of a loving person to notice the subtle changes, communicate, and adapt. The goal is to take the necessary steps to meet the current needs and thereby continue to make the other person feel loved and valued. It is during these times of change that we either lose touch or stay connected in our hearts. It is often during the times that have so much potential for disaster that we can make quantum leaps forward in the depths of love, trust, and respect.

All it takes to win your mate's trust and affection is an acknowledgment that things have changed.

All it takes to win your mate's trust and affection is an acknowledgment that things have changed. Just the fact that you notice is impressive! For instance, when I am at a certain point in a project, whether it be writing a book or studying for a ministry trip, Brenda has always worked a strategy to help me feel less pressure and be more creative, without my asking.

There were times I would notice that the kids were not at home. When I inquired why, I usually heard, "I knew you would be studying and would need a lot of time alone." I could hardly believe my ears. Sometimes I hadn't even thought that far in advance. But it was such a blessing!

After you notice the changes, communicate. Ask the questions that will help you find out what is important to your mate at that moment. When I am working, I will sometimes forget to eat. When I do, I get nauseated and have to stop working. I lose a lot of creativity during the downtime. Without my asking her, Brenda often will show up at my study with food. She knows that I will wait too long to eat. She, however, is just the opposite; when she works she doesn't want to stop to eat. If I brought her food, it would be wasted and unappreciated time and effort.

Many of the changes we go through are temporary. However, if we fail to properly adapt to change, it can cause irreversible damage. I have seen divorces that had been building for twenty years, starting after the birth of the first child. I have seen a couple's sex life destroyed by what happened on the honeymoon.

The Bottom Line: God Loves Us

For several months I casually asked people what they thought the deepest need of a husband or wife might be. Most of the answers were what I call "fruit" answers, not "root" answers. Fruit is the perceived need; it is not the real need. But it is what the person thinks he or she needs. The "root" is the real need. For example, a person may say, "I want my wife to show me more respect." That is actually a fruit need. The root need is a better sense of self-worth.

Our deepest need is to be loved.

At the root of our deepest need is simply the need to be loved. Everything else is somewhat superficial. The need for consistent *agape*-love can be met ultimately only in a relationship with a loving God. He is the only Being with the quality of love that is unconditional and unwavering. Thus, He must be our source of love.

Because *agape* is about value, it also is the source of self-worth. When we discover and believe the great value that God has for us, which He expressed through the death, burial, and resurrection of Jesus, we are able to gain a sense of worth that is constant and abiding. People are able to respond properly in any situation only when they have a sense of self-worth based on the love of God. No one and nothing else can fully meet that need.

Yet God created us in such a way that we also would experience love through our relationship with our mates. He was the One who said, *"It is not good for the man to be alone"* (Genesis 2:18 NIV). The union that God would create between man and woman would become the closest parallel to God's relationship with mankind. Our ability to walk in love and develop our relationship with our mates would be a gauge to help us understand where we are spiritually. As mankind has destroyed the concepts of family, fatherhood, and marriage, we have lost that sense of God's relationship with man.

There is no greater gauge for true spirituality than our ability to share in loving relationships. The apostle John pointed out,

> *If someone says, "I love God," and hates his brother, he is a liar; for he who does not love his brother whom he has seen, how can he love God whom he has not seen? And this commandment we have from Him: that he who loves God must love his brother also.* (1 John 4:20–21 NKJV)

How much more should we *agape*-love our mates? Yet we allow ourselves to drift away. It is as if we come to a fork in the road and don't notice that our mates take the other fork. Then one day we turn around and wonder why we don't feel close. The truth is that we aren't even walking the same path.

At every turn in the road, at every new change, we want to maintain love for one another. The young pregnant wife wonders, "Will I be precious to my husband when I am too uncomfortable to have sex? Will he still think I'm

beautiful when I gain fifty pounds?" The middle-aged man questions, "Will she still want me when I am bald?" It is when these questions go unanswered that fear gives way to withheld emotions. Again, when we do not feel special or valued, we do not feel (*agape*) loved. When we do not feel loved, we will not respond with affection and passion. It is these unanswered questions that create the mid-life crisis and the empty nest syndrome. All of the destructive, dysfunctional ventures we follow instead are vain pursuits to find someone who will give us value and acceptance.

> At every change in life, needs and expectations of both partners change. It is the mark of a loving person to notice the subtle changes, communicate, and adapt.

I Almost Lost Everything

As Brenda and I reached one of these critical junctures, it brought us both to unknown territory. For the first time in our lives we weren't struggling to pay bills. Our kids were nearly grown, and things had changed for the better. Yet it was one of the loneliest periods in our lives. We both found ourselves doing things that were hurtful to the other. It seemed that an unseen hand was leading our marriage to destruction, and we didn't know how to break free from its grasp.

I remember how, as we sat in a restaurant, we had to face this "monster" or lose the most precious thing we had. It was Brenda's favorite restaurant. We ordered our favorite food. But when it was set before us, I could only sit and stare at the plate. I couldn't eat. I couldn't speak for fear of crying. Nothing major had happened to bring us to this point. Neither of us could really put a finger on one thing and say, "This is the heart of the problem." Yet we were in trouble.

I finally broke the silence. Straining to fight back the tears, I said, "I feel like I'm losing you. I feel like you're slipping through my fingers." With very few words, she acknowledged the same feelings. I felt like I would die. For a few days after that I did want to die. I could not face this. I could not lose what had been so very precious to me. I didn't want to simply stay married; I wanted to recapture the passion and romance that had fueled our lives for so many years.

Over the next few weeks, the situation changed very little. We spoke a little more nicely to each other, we tried a little harder, but it was all a great effort in futility. Neither of us really knew what to say. One day I walked home from the office in the middle of the day. I walked into the laundry room and found Brenda sitting on the floor crying. I had very rarely seen her cry in our entire married life. Still, I knew this cry came from someplace so deep that it was impossible to touch with mere words. It was the cry of a broken heart.

I took her in my arms and held her. I didn't ask what was wrong. She could never explain it, and neither could I. Everything was just different. It was beyond words. Although everything in our lives was going better than it ever had, everything had changed, and we had drifted out of touch. We had not adapted to the changes in our lives, and we were losing our connection. I knew I was no longer touching her heart.

As I held her in my arms, I repented. I didn't repent about a specific sin or doing her a wrong. Rather, I changed my mind about where I would place my priorities. I readjusted my values. Too often we sacrifice our relationships because we can justify our actions. If we're not really doing anything wrong, why should we have to change? Simple—because it's not working!

When Brenda and I were first married, we were very poor. We struggled to make ends meet. I was fighting my way through a life-threatening illness with no medical insurance. We faced days when our children didn't have enough food for lunch. There were times when I didn't have enough gas to drive to work. I had creditors calling my house and pounding on my door. Yet we were so happy. None of those things could hurt us very deeply. Our hearts were protected by our love for one another.

If we aren't doing anything wrong, why should we have to change? Simple—because it's not working!

I worked hard to get out of debt and make a good life. I did all that I knew I should do, but in the process I stopped touching her heart. The process became more consuming than the person I loved. Now I was losing the love of the woman who had motivated me to take those steps. I was losing the woman for whom I was putting forth all this effort. I was gaining the world and losing the love of my life. I don't think you have to make a choice between the two, but we chose love over all else.

That day I determined that I would do everything I could to make Brenda feel safe and special. At that point there wasn't a need to go back and try to figure out who did what. I just knew that my wife didn't feel safe and special anymore. I knew I was no longer touching her heart with the love that had once made her feel so special. We had lost our connection. There were events that I could have looked at and said, "You did this." But she could have done the same. I didn't want to win an argument; I wanted to win her heart.

Before you continue reading, maybe you need to ask yourself, "Is it a high priority for me that my mate feel safe and special? What am I doing to make that happen? Am I paying attention to his or her needs? Are my mate's needs as important as my own? Am I really touching my mate's heart with my love?"

Repentance is when you change your mind. Maybe you need to change your mind about where you are putting your time, attention, and effort!

Chapter II

False Expectations

Chapter II

False Expectations

We all enter marriage with certain expectations. Each of us has our own ideas of what types of pleasure this new step will bring into our lives. Sadly, we do not discuss these expectations with our prospective mates. They may have no idea what we are expecting. Nonetheless, we assume they should know. We assume that everyone views marriage and its roles the same way. And when these expectations do not come to pass, our feelings can range from disappointment to anger and betrayal. Sometimes we feel that the other person has broken a promise to us! Too often the pain of failed expectations is unrealistic. When someone fails to meet our expectations, although it feels like he or she broke a promise, that is very often not the case. Very simply, expectations that have not been communicated and agreed upon should not be expected.

Talk—Don't Assume

Expectation without communication takes us to the place of judgment. Judgment comes when we assume we know "why" a person does what he or she does. When we have an expectation that is not fulfilled, our first response is usually to assume why. We come up with our own reason of why it didn't happen. Rarely do we include in our judgment the fact that we never had a commitment from the person! We usually assume that he or she didn't fulfill our expectations deliberately to hurt us. Or we think that person really doesn't love us. The list of such judgments is endless. Many marriage conflicts, especially those that occur in the first few years, are based on false expectations.

About fifty percent of all the people who have ever come to me for premarital counseling decided not to get married. That may seem like a high number to you, but that is about the same percentage of people who will get divorced. How does the premarital counseling I provide help people make that decision before the hurt is compounded by a marriage commitment? It doesn't have any real secret formulas. It simply gets people to discuss the areas of their expectations. I have these prospective couples talk about what most people don't discuss until after they are married.

You see, we assume that the "love of our life" feels the same way about things that we do. We think because we agree on "this," we will automatically agree on "that." And when we discover that our expectations are not going to be fulfilled—usually after marriage—we often feel cheated and deceived.

The male view of marriage seems to be something like this: "I am the man. I am the head of the house. That means I will make all the decisions." That also means any misunderstandings that the couple has automatically default to his point of view. "I am the man; I am right." That bubble gets busted pretty quickly.

I recall a couple who had different backgrounds and different ideas. She had been successful in business and had a good track record at handling finances. He convinced her that, biblically, her role was to yield to him in every decision. His track record with money was horrible. Once he got control of the household money, her credit was ruined, and they both had to file bankruptcy.

If he had been walking in *agape*-love, he would have had value for her background and respected her success. He would have been able to defer to her and learn from her. Instead he used the Scriptures to manipulate his agenda.

Communication is the way safety and confidence are established.

The marriage ended in divorce, and she was questioning God's Word because of the way it had been used to manipulate the situation.

As we talked she said, "I didn't know it was going to be like this. I thought we were going to be a team!" They both went into the marriage with expectations that had not been discussed. Those failed expectations compounded the pain of the financial failure and added to the strain that ultimately brought about their divorce.

If *agape*-love is about value and preciousness, then it stands to reason that we would never force anyone to do what he or she does not want to do. Neither should we disregard the person's experience and intelligence. The moment force is brought into the picture, feelings of personal worth begin to suffer. Distrust begins to grow. The ability to respond with feelings of affection and passion dissipates.

Communication is the way safety and confidence are established. "Safe" communication is the precursor to openness, and safe communication occurs when communication rules are established and observed. Some of the essential rules could include these: Never attack. Never pass a judgment. If you want to know why, ask. Never touch the other person's self-worth. Always show respect for the other person and his or her point of view. Every couple may have different communication rules. Decide what makes you feel safe when you communicate. Have your spouse do the same, and together create a "Communication Agreement."

In order for both parties to enjoy safe communication, there must be no aggression. Keep in mind that what you call aggression may not be what your mate calls aggression. The only way to know what makes your spouse feel unsafe is to ask. Asking questions is essential for success in all forms of communication. When you are willing to adjust your communication style to make your mate feel safe, you have proven how precious he or she is to you. You are laying the foundation for loving, trusting responses that can flow forth for a lifetime.

I often tell the story about discussing my expectations with Brenda before we were married. I love getting a good start in the morning. The morning is the time of day when I can be productive. I accomplish so much more in the mornings. So, my mornings are important.

Two things that were very important to me were that I have clean, ironed clothes to select an outfit from and that I eat a good meal. (When my eyes are open, I am usually hungry.) I dress for my own inspiration. I don't wear the same thing on any particular day. It is all about what I am going to be doing, what I want to accomplish, and how I want to feel. So I don't want just a clean set of clothes. I want a choice.

I am also one of those people who, when hungry, gets very fidgety, sometimes dizzy, and unpleasant. If I go too long without eating, it can take me a full day to recover physical strength. So eating is important to the success of my day!

Brenda was completely agreeable to making sure that I had clothes to wear, but she did not want to cook breakfast. She is not a morning person. The smell of food in the morning is nauseating for her, and she really doesn't like to talk in the mornings.

I could have pressured her into making my breakfast. I could have made her feel obligated. But

Discussing and coming to terms with every expectation will make it possible to avoid the majority of marital friction.

because I value her feelings, I was willing to get up and cook my own breakfast. A person could argue about the duties of a wife yadda, yadda, yadda ad nauseum! But while that guy is fighting with his wife every day, I am enjoying my time alone in the mornings, I have a passionate romantic marriage, and I am reaping incredible benefits in others areas.

When Brenda told me that she did not want to cook in the morning, I did not retaliate or resort to pressure. I also made sure she didn't feel guilty about it. I respect her wishes, just as she respects mine.

Resolving the Expectation Conflict

When Brenda and I got married, we had very few surprises with one another. We discussed what we expected. We made agreements, and we have lived by those agreements. They are changed only by a willing agreement between us. Time does dictate that agreements change. As our lives have changed, many of the things that were important are no longer important. Many things that were not important then are far more important now. Continual safe communication makes it possible for us to recognize, discuss, and adapt to our new needs.

But you may object, "What if something is really important to me that my mate doesn't want to do?" That is very often the reason some of those fifty percent of premarital counselees stop their weddings. They realize that they will not be happy because of the differences in values. Remember, a large enough difference in values will cause someone to not feel *agape*-love. And without *agape*, the other forms of love will not emerge.

Continual safe communication makes it possible for us to recognize, discuss, and adapt to our new needs.

Ultimately, we must realize that if something is so important to us, we should be willing to do it for ourselves. If we are not willing to do it for ourselves, but we want our mates to do it, it must not be essential. If it is unrealistic that we could do it, it may be a reason not to get married. We can't get married with the idea that we will eventually wear the person down, that he or she will eventually succumb to the pressure and do what we want.

It is essential to realize you cannot expect or require people to do anything that violates the Word of God, compromises their will or conscience, or diminishes their self-worth. These are absolute lines that must never be crossed.

A number of men and women in counseling complain about their sex life. They feel that they have a great sex life, but every time one partner allows passion to flow freely, the other tries to force him or her into something he or she does not want to do. Besides the fact that it destroys the moment, it also creates a dread of sexual intimacy. Plus, the idea that your mate could try to coerce you into something you do not want completely undermines respect and self-worth.

Discussing and coming to terms with every expectation will make it possible for you to avoid the majority of all marital friction. You can live your life in prevention and even healing. On the other hand, if you do not communicate and reach meaningful agreements, you will live in frustration and bitterness. Your life will be full of conflict—the conflict that emerges from failed expectations or from trying to force your will on your mate. Either way, there will be conflict.

Some of the greatest conflicts occur between people who have been married for years and who have never discussed expectations. Let me give you some advice: It is never too late to have this discussion. Don't avoid this discussion because you fear it will only produce conflict. Momentary conflict is better than a life of hurt and disappointment. The disappointment of unfulfilled desires and the disappointment of being pressured into something you never agreed to are both equally painful. Many times the couples who have been married the longest without this type of discussion are the ones who are hurting the most.

Sit down today with your mate or mate-to-be and discuss your expectations. Let him or her know what is important to you. Find out if there are things you have imposed on your spouse without his or her agreement. Discover where there are gaps in your concepts and expectations. If you have been married for a while, this could be embarrassing or even hurtful. It may be wise to establish some communication rules before you have this or any other serious discussion. It is never to late to bring the dignity of free choice to your marriage. Your mate will love and respect you for the effort, especially if your mate is the one who has had expectations forced upon him or her.

This also would be a great time to make a list of the top five things that make each of you feel loved. Then swap lists and get ready to step into a new era of life and marriage. After you work on that list for a few weeks, make a list of the top five things your mate does that makes you feel unloved. Swap lists again and take another huge leap forward in the world of *agape*-love.

Chapter 12

Don't Force It

Chapter 12

Don't Force It

The amount of violence in the world is growing by leaps and bounds. The growth of violence in the streets, however, is the product of increasing violence in the home. Unreasonable and selfish people are considering violence to be an acceptable option for reaching their goals. Because it is modeled at home, it becomes a way of life very early.

Breeding violence does not require physical abuse. On the contrary, violence emerges from *force*. Force is simply a subtle form of violence. When there is force, no one is physically struck, but the same emotions are inflicted on the victim: fear, intimidation, and shame. On the part of the perpetrator there is a show of power, strength, and superiority. Violence is part of the same continuum as force. Force is simply a lesser degree of the same intention. It is more socially acceptable because it does not produce physical pain or leave marks on a body, but it emerges from the same intentions and attitudes as violence. Once the concept of force is accepted, the groundwork is laid for violence. It subtly grows from one to the other.

Force can be shown by a woman who withholds sex from her husband in order to get him to do something he would not normally do. It is force when a man withholds finances to make his wife do what she does not want to do. I can remember my father coming home late at night drunk. He would want my mother to get up and cook for him. Even if he did not use violence, he argued, nagged, and coerced until she got out of bed and made him a meal in the middle of the night.

There are all kinds of ways to exert force. The key factor is that one person uses pressure or power of some kind to get another person to do what he or she would not willingly do.

Subtle Forms of Force

Force takes people's freedoms from them. It says, "You have no choice." It strips people of their sense of dignity. One of the common emotional struggles of people who have been robbed is shame. Shame, in turn, robs dignity. Without dignity, there is no sense of value. And without value there is no sense of being loved (*agape*). Force has the same effect as robbery.

Although some would never resort to open force or physical abuse, they would, nonetheless, feel quite comfortable entering the subtle realms of manipulation and coercion. Manipulation is merely a more socially acceptable form of force and violence. Whether it is emotional manipulation, physical force, or violent abuse, the end result is the same. A person is made to do something he or she did not choose. One person had to give up his or her will to another.

In Galatians 3:1 Paul identified control as a form of witchcraft. Control is the goal of sorcery; it is "bewitching" someone to get that person to act contrary to his or her will.

Control, however, is not accomplished through potions or magic spells. It is done by intimidation, manipulation, guilt, or other negative means.

When we get people to act contrary to their will, we are in fact taking their lives away from them. It is a subtle form of murder. That is the goal of the murderer: to take a person's life. That is also the goal of the controller. However subtle it may be, taking any part of a person's life is a bold declaration of our lack of value for his or her life.

Thelma was in just such a situation. Her husband had never beaten her or raised a hand to her; but after more than twenty-five years of marriage, she was finished. All of her family and friends were surprised. She had always seemed like such a cooperative, agreeable type.

As we talked, she shared that she had never been "allowed" to live any of her personal dreams. Her husband always made her feel that her dreams were not important. He always had subtle, intimidating ways to discourage her from doing what she wanted with her life. So she quietly raised her children and then left. She refused to go to her grave living a life she did not choose.

The force her husband used was not brutal. It was just enough to get his way, to steal her dreams, to take her life. She didn't want anything outrageous. She simply wanted to do something for God. Over the years this control and subtle manipulation robbed her of any love and respect for her husband. They hadn't kissed in years.

Both parties in a marriage need to make an absolute commitment to abstain from force of any kind. Peace, safety, and choice facilitate an environment that allows for affection and passion to flourish. They engender trust and openness.

As an adult I have been a communicator and a problem solver. When things went wrong, I was ready to work it out right then. No need to wait around; just get to it! I was quite comfortable thinking out loud, facing objections, and even arguing something through if that's what it took. I actually was a little self-righteous in my great willingness to communicate.

Brenda, on the other hand, is one who wants to think it through before she talks. She needs time to process her emotions. Verbalizing her deep thoughts is somewhat threatening to her. She came from a background of physical abuse where it was not safe to say what you felt, especially if you were disagreeing.

I have never abused her, I intellectualized, *so there is no logical reason she should withhold communication from me.* So being the wise peacemaker that I am, when there was a problem, I pressed to work it out; I was being open and communicative. It was during this time that I had to learn a new phrase: "I'm not ready to talk about it!" You would think I would have understood. All of these initials after my name should have brought me something of value. But I didn't get it!

Even when you want to do the "right thing," there is no room for force on any level. Because of past experiences, talking through issues was very threatening for Brenda. Her experience said that this type of conversation always leads to physical abuse. She knew that I would not abuse her, but her emotions still paralyzed her. Many times I pressed for communication. I was sure it would "help."

Instead it only served to take small conflicts and make them into major ones.

Refusing to Use Force

I came to realize that the meaning of communication is not determined by the one speaking. Rather, it means what it means to the listener. For Brenda, "let's talk" meant "let's fight." For her, "let's talk" was aggression. It brought fear and anxiety. My reasonable attempts to solve a problem when she was not ready was a form of force since force is using power to make someone do what he or she does not choose to do. My intention did not change her experience. All control is a form of force. Again, force is on the same continuum as violence, and violence destroys love. Therefore, one of my laws of love and communication says, "My intention does not define my action. The other person's experience defines my action."

Peace, safety, and choice facilitate an environment that allows for affection and passion to flourish. They engender trust and openness.

I determined that I would win Brenda's trust. I wanted her to experience the freedom of communication without fear. I wanted her to know what it was like to have love rather than pain grow out of disagreements.

I determined that I would never respond to her in any negative way, no matter what she said. Keep in mind that to a fearful person, even objectivity can feel very negative and aggressive. If I disagreed with her, I determined that I would wait a day or two and then come back to her to discuss my concern. The key was that she would never meet with any aggression when she attempted to communicate.

I stuck to my plan...for three years. After about three years, she grew in her trust for me to a place where now we can talk about almost anything. Now I am able to express myself to her, disagree with her, and even argue without it being a terribly traumatic experience for either of us. She feels safe with me.

During those three years I had the opportunity to develop areas of self-control and positive communication that I never would have discovered otherwise. There was no other area of my life where I had enough value for anyone to face those kinds of challenges. Some would ask, "Don't you think three years is too long of a time to deal with something like this?" Well, we could have fought for a few years and then lived in rejection and torment. We both could have backslidden in our anger and disappointment. We could have embittered our children and gotten a divorce. Then we could have dragged all that hurt into another marriage and faced the same problem all over again. We probably could have spent between five and ten years in such a process. No, those three years were one of the best investments I have ever made. It was time well spent!

When you marry someone, you marry his or her past. Do you have enough value for your spouse to help him or her outgrow the past?

When you marry someone, you marry all of that person's past. The person's previous pain is sort of like a credit card debt that you help him or her pay off after you get married. You didn't spend the money. You didn't create the bill. But you make the payments. The question is, do you have enough value for your spouse to help him or her "pay off" the past? Are you willing to face your own issues that will arise as a result of refusing to resort to force? Are you willing to grow into the person you need to be so your mate can grow into the person he or she can be?[12]

Here at Impact Ministries we tell our leaders that they can never use negative motivation to get anyone to do anything. Everyone loves that when he or she first hears it. "This is great! We're going to work in a positive environment." After about a year, a new leader starts getting discouraged and negativity begins to creep out. Then you usually hear, "It is so hard to get these people to do anything." Then I remind the leader, "No, it is not hard to get these people to do anything. What is hard is finding ways to motivate people when the use of force is not an option."

Coercion is such a part of life that we know very little about how to work with people without it—especially in our homes and among the people we are with every day. Yet, nothing will endear someone to you as much as freedom of choice and feelings of safety.

Do you consider force of any kind to be a reasonable option to get what you want? What type of force, or pressure, do you tend to use when you want something from your mate? What are you attempting to get your mate to do that he or she does not want to do? If it is something that should happen, what positive, creative ways can you employ to show your mate the value it will bring to the relationship? This would be a good time to acknowledge, to your mate, the ways you have used force in the past, apologize and then assure him or her that they will no longer be a part of your relationship.

---

[12] Please understand that in no way am I advocating that you stay in a violent situation. Nor am I saying you should enable a codependency. I am simply saying that you should recognize that force is not an option when building a loving relationship.

Chapter 13

The Safety Net

Chapter 13

The Safety Net

We all want to know that we have a safety net. I don't mind taking certain risks—I just want to know that, if I fall, there's a net. When I was a young boy, I lied about my age and got a job as a construction worker. I was a boilermaker. We built water tanks, housings for nuclear reactors, and other large steel structures. I was terribly afraid of heights, but I was willing to work several hundred feet in the air if there was at least a safety rope. Such is life. We will climb to the greatest heights if we know there is a net waiting below to catch us!

Walking in love is very threatening territory. It is like climbing an extremely high structure. Telling you how I really feel, expressing how your actions are really affecting me, owning my own weaknesses, giving you my heart fully—that is very risky business. The degree of honesty and vulnerability that is required for this kind of relationship is far beyond what most are willing to risk...unless they have a safety net.

This safety net is the degree of trust I have for you. I must know it is safe for me to give you this much of my life before I am willing to take the plunge. On the other hand, most of us expect our mates to blindly leap into our arms.

They should know that we love them, and they should just trust us!

Creating the Safety Net of Trust

Trust, however, is never given; it is earned. The person who gives unearned trust will be hurt repeatedly. Of course, we must always be *willing* to trust. *Agape*-love should not look for reasons to withhold trust. But we should trust only to the level that someone has proven trustworthiness. Even God doesn't ask us to trust beyond the level of love He has proven.

Trust is also given in specific areas. I may trust you to provide, but can I trust you to be generous? I may trust you with the part of my dreams that is rational and logical. But can I trust you with the part of my dreams that is far beyond my reach? Will you encourage me or make fun of me? Can I trust you to encourage me even when it will not be convenient for you?

Trust is never given; it is earned. Even God doesn't ask us to trust beyond the level of love He has proven.

We must never demand trust. Rather, we should seek to understand where and why our spouses trust us. And we should seek to understand where and why they do not trust us. Rarely will a person tell you his or her areas of mistrust. If it were safe enough to tell you the area, the person would probably already trust you in that area. This is where patient observation and non-threatening communication will win over the most fearful heart.

You must remember that every time you are gentle and patient with your spouse in an area that is potentially threatening and unsafe, you send an unspoken message of value (*agape*). I can't tell you how many times my wife has told me how special it made her feel when I was patient with her in an area where she had a lot of uncertainty.

In reality, your kindness and patience—both qualities of *agape*-love—forge the trust that becomes the safety net. You see, a marriage license is not proof that you will stay married. Being a Christian is not proof that you will walk in love. Reading the Bible is not proof you will do what it says. Saying you will understand is not proof that you do. The only proof a person can trust is your track record—and it takes time to build a track record. Once you have seriously failed in an area, it takes time to rebuild a new track record.

Until you have established a new track record, it is idealistic and naïve for you to expect anyone to trust you. If you

> Your acts of faithfulness become ropes woven together to form the safety net of trust that your spouse needs.

demand trust and openness, your very actions prove that you are not trustworthy. As a matter of fact, the less you demand and the less force or pressure you use, the more you become safe and trustworthy. Your acts of faithfulness become ropes woven together to form the safety net of trust that your spouse needs.

Safety must be an agreed-upon goal. You both must be committed to making the other person feel safe. Naturally, that should start with physical safety. Physical attack of any kind can never be tolerated in any relationship. There is no justification for physical attack.

A part of physical safety includes provision. This is especially important to a wife and mother: "Will my husband provide for our family? Will he be sure that the basic needs of our family are provided?" When the husband or wife excessively or impulsively spends, he or she is

creating an unsafe environment. Financial pressures top the list for marriage conflicts. Many areas of sexual dysfunction are linked to financial pressures. This is an area where there needs to be honest communication and joint planning.

Very often a husband will say, "I'm the one who goes out and works for the money, so I should make all the decisions about how it is spent." Usually when that happens, I help the wife calculate what all of her services would cost; after all, if he wants to make it an issue of earning wages, we'll beat him with his own logic. Most men find they could never pay someone for all the childcare, cleaning, shopping, cooking, office work, errands, and sex, just to mention a few.

> A marriage license is not proof that you will stay married. Reading the Bible is not proof you will do what it says. The only proof a person can trust is your track record.

When it is a simple case of being unaware, the man very quickly apologizes and includes his wife in the financial planning. When it is a case of greed and control, I'll hear an argument that continues to express his lack of value and respect for his wife and family. This man is usually headed for divorce and doesn't see it coming.

Where most people do not feel safe is in the area of emotions. There must be no emotional control, attack, manipulation, or intimidation in this area. We must each, within reason, be allowed to process our issues the way that works for us. We talk about things only when we are both ready to talk about them.

To ensure emotional safety, there must be value for the other person's point of view. I cannot count the number of couples whose marriages are failing today because one or both do not listen to the other. Men are notorious for not listening to their wives. I discovered something in that area that is worth its weight in gold: "My wife may not know about business, but she knows about me." More importantly, my wife feels safe expressing what she sees.

Build Trust in Every Area

When we were facing incredibly difficult financial pressure, I found a business idea that I thought would help us get out of debt. Brenda and I sat down and discussed it in detail. It would require that I work late nearly every night, which meant that I would not be with the family in the evenings. I was not willing to make those kinds of changes without her agreement. We agreed that I would come home in the afternoon to be with the kids, then go back out to work. She would then get the kids in bed so that we would have some private time together when I came home between 9 and 10 p.m. We agreed that if the business did not do what we expected in one year, I would get out.

If I had walked in, announced my plans, and given her no voice in the matter, she probably would have gone along. She probably would have made the best of it, but there would have been considerable loss of love and trust. She would not have felt emotionally safe with me; it would have seemed her feelings were not important to me.

I have never gone into any business venture that would affect our family without complete agreement with my wife. There have been times I have come home with an idea. More than once it has been a "sure thing." I've known it was something that I could do and create good finances. More than once she has said, "I don't want to do this." I reasoned back, "But, honey, you just don't understand this opportunity." Her response goes something like this: "I may not understand the opportunity, but I understand you. This is what you will do if you get in this business. I don't like the way this will affect our life." I would rather lose money than lose my wife's trust and love. More money can't buy what we have!

I am amazed when I see men make major changes in jobs—moving to different cities or starting new business ventures—without ever considering how it will affect their families. Just because you are the breadwinner doesn't give you the right to change everything in your spouse's life without her consent. Maybe she would rather maintain the current level of income and stay with family and friends in the current location.

Great sex can't happen if both parties do not feel completely safe.

I see people make all kinds of major life-altering decisions without the agreement of their mates. Agreement, by the way, is not selling your spouse on the idea; agreement is when it is something he or she wants, too. Many divorces occur within years of major life changes. The change may have improved your financial status, may have put you in a new house; but was it done in a way that cost your mate what he or she valued? You must safeguard the emotions, values, and concerns of your mate in every decision.

One of the places where few people feel truly safe is the bedroom. Self-worth and ego are incredibly fragile when it comes to sex; this may be the most emotionally volatile area of a person's life. That is why it requires complete safety. Great sex can't happen if both parties do not feel completely safe. If any force or coercion is displayed in even the smallest amount, the bedroom will never be safe or fulfilling.

If you are going to be the safety net your mate needs, there is no place you can't go, no issue you can't face, no problem you can't discuss, and no adventure you can't explore. Yet let there be one hint of selfishness, and the doors of trust will begin to close. When there is no trust, there is no safety net. And when there is no safety net, your mate will not climb to new heights of life with you!

There are some questions you must ask before you move ahead. Ask yourself, "Does my mate feel safe with me physically, emotionally, and sexually? Is his or her safety a priority to me? Is it reflected in my words, tone of voice, and actions? What can I do to make our relationship more safe?" Make a list of what you discover and include it in your daily prayer time. God will empower you to walk in love once you commit yourself to do it.

Chapter 14

Safe Sex

Chapter 14

Safe Sex

Safe sex for a married couple is not about protection from disease; it is about protection from fear. In order to have passionate sexual intimacy—which is the desire of every married couple—there must be complete freedom from fear. Of all the areas in which there must be safety, sexual intimacy is the most essential and the most volatile. This is the area in which nearly every couple needs more honesty and communication.

The fears that are stirred when people begin to venture into sexual intimacy are some of the deepest. Our sexual lives can be the source of great confidence or the place where our egos are shattered. It is probably the most threatening place for the male ego when things are not going well; and it is the source of shame and disgrace for many women.

Surprisingly, it is all the events leading up to the bedroom that most determine if it is a safe place—not just the events that take place in the bedroom. The level of trust in other areas, the way we solve problems, and how we communicate form the backdrop of trust that we take to the bedroom. If there is no trust in these areas, it is unlikely

that trust will be given in the area of sexual intimacy. If people feel safe sexually, they can give themselves wholly to sexual intimacy. Passion can flow freely. If they do not feel safe, satisfaction is always beyond their reach.

Many of the things that determine your mate's sense of safety may have little to do with you. Remember, the person you have married, or are going to marry, is the sum total of his or her life experiences up to that point. Your spouse's ability to respond to you is based on past experiences as much as it is on present experiences.

Brenda and I had an incredible amount of passion for one another. Yet we still had many issues to overcome in order for us to have a great sex life. She had experienced sex without intimacy in the past. The bedroom had never been a safe place for her; instead, it was a place where she was forced to prove herself, and she brought that pain with her into our marriage. On the other hand, I had little value for sex without intimacy. My early life of debauchery had shown me that sex apart from a committed relationship was sexually unsatisfying and emotionally destructive, and I didn't want that!

Brenda's past experience said that if someone shows intimacy, he wants sex. That meant she would resist intimacy unless she was in the mood for sex. (Her rejection of intimacy was very difficult for me. Because I was aware of her past, however, I knew that her rejection wasn't about me; it was about what she feared.) On top of that, if she refused my advances for intimacy, she feared I would retaliate with violence. All of this added to the confusion of the moment, but this was what her past experience had been. I could not demand that she change all that. Intellectually, she knew that was not our reality; emotionally, though, it felt the same.

Intimacy First, Then Sex

I have heard probably hundreds of women complain, "I want my husband to be more affectionate." His reply is, "When I am affectionate, you reject me." Then she explains, "That's because the only time you are affectionate is when you want sex." It is an endless cycle of fear, pain, and rejection. When a fight breaks out, it reinforces the association of emotional conflict and sex. For many couples, sex is an obligation that is done as a duty. They never break out of the pain and enjoy sexual intimacy on the level that God intended.

Safe intimacy is one of the keys to creating safe sex. Sex without intimacy is like having sex with a prostitute. It is what makes one feel dirty. It cheapens the entire experience. Maybe we should all ask, "What is it I really want when I have sex?" If you just want to be gratified, you are not a candidate for an incredible lifetime of great sex. If you want to have intimacy and emotional connection, you are on the right path.

A lifetime of personal experience, study, and counseling has shown me that the only people who experience incredible depths of sexual gratification as God intended are those who are devoted to the emotional and physical satisfaction of their mates. These people are committed to *agape*-love. They value their mates' feelings and are committed to protecting those feelings in every arena of life, especially in this, the most vulnerable of all areas.

The spouse who is committed to the gratification of the other person has to pay attention. This spouse doesn't advance any part of the "sexual play" until his or her mate is responding wholeheartedly at the present level of activity.

Some of the greatest manuscripts ever written about foreplay teach men to recognize the different levels of arousal of their wives and not to move forward until their mates have been adequately stimulated.

Sometimes the greatest level of gratification for my mate means that I do not extend the foreplay to intercourse. If her level of arousal doesn't progress, I should notice and not try to get her to go beyond where she is physically and emotionally prepared to go. The way I solved this problem was by a simple commitment; I decided, "I will never initiate sex."

> The only people who experience the incredible depths of sexual gratification as God intended are those who are committed to the emotional and physical satisfaction of their mates.

When people first hear me say this, they are quite taken back, especially men. Then I have to clarify. I never initiate *sex*. I initiate *intimacy* and *romance*. How Brenda responds tells me how far we need to go. I want her to know I have so much value for her that I can reach any level of arousal and will gladly stop if she is not ready to proceed.

Because I have learned how to experience love, I know I can kiss her, hold her in my arms, and be very satisfied. We can experience more passion by holding each other than we can by having sex that we are not both ready to wholeheartedly commit to.

The Key Is the Emotional Connection

There are incredible benefits to this approach. First, when my wife and I do make love, it is always good. When we make love, we connect emotionally; it is not a mere

physical experience. We connect in a way that fortifies our relationship. We feel good about each other. We preserve dignity and respect. Then, because Brenda trusts me so much in this area, she is looking and noticing my needs. If she senses that my passions are high, she will initiate romance. I can't put into words how loved it makes me feel to know that she notices and cares about my needs. When there is trust and respect, life becomes a romantic reciprocation of intimacy on every level.

When there is trust and respect, life becomes a romantic reciprocation of intimacy on every level.

Because we both feel safe, we can give ourselves to the moment. As was discussed earlier, for there to be *eros*, there must be the freedom to give yourself fully and completely to your passion. You must feel free emotionally in order to focus on and experience the moment. Because Brenda and I have no fears, we can enjoy the moment. We can connect. Contrary to popular opinion, great sex is not based on how wild it is. Great sex can be wild and passionate, yes, but it also can be sweet and tender. The thing that gives sex value and makes it great is the emotional connection. We want to come together and experience oneness both physically and emotionally.

There are many reasons a person may not give him- or herself to the moment. I often find in counseling that one member of the husband-wife team does not allow the other to enjoy the moment. He or she rushes straight to intercourse without the pleasure of preparation. But the person's approach to the process determines if the moment will be one of blissful romance or physical sex. Another reason some people do not give themselves to the moment, as mentioned in a previous chapter, is for fear of being manipulated.

Whatever you must do to make it possible, learn to enjoy every moment of the sexual process. Most of that enjoyment comes through the emotional connection and sensitivity that puts you and your spouse in the same moment at the same time.

One of the incredible things that happens to people who are in sync emotionally is a parallel "in sync" in their sex drive. Unless there are physical problems, couples who emotionally connect seem to flow in and out of their desire for sex at the same times. When I begin to have sexual stirrings, I know that I need not be impatient; Brenda will usually begin to move into the same heightened desire very soon. She experiences the same thing with me. And when we are not highly sexually motivated, we still maintain a bond of intimacy. We still kiss even when we are not sexually stimulated. (And we connect when we kiss!)

Does your mate feel safe enough to give him- or herself completely to sexual intimacy? Or has your lifestyle convinced your spouse that it is not intimacy you want? Are you willing to listen and respond to your mate's need for safety? Talk to your mate about his or her feelings of safety in intimacy. Ask how you can make it more safe and enjoyable. Ask if there is anything you should stop doing because it has a negative effect on the moment.

Chapter 15

I Need to Be Needed

Chapter 15

I Need to Be Needed

There is a "vaccination" that will keep you from ever experiencing real love. It is so painless, most people don't even know when they have been inoculated. They just spend the rest of their lives wondering why love never finds them.

I once heard John Osteen say, "Religion is like a vaccination. It gives you just enough of the real thing so you can't get it!" I have since learned that every area of life, especially relationships, has these vaccinations. (Religion is just one example!) Vaccinations are part reality and part deceit. They are just the right mixture to create an immunity to the real thing, be it love or relationships.

Brenda and I recently started weight training together. I had done this type of exercise on and off for years, so I had a lot of experience at what would work and what would not. After a while she began to complain, "I'm working out more than you are, but you're getting better results." When I observed her workout routine, I saw that she was not using proper form. Now, she really was working out; she was dedicated and determined. Unless she adjusted her approach, however, she would not get what she sought. In the end she would have become discouraged and quit. This was a type of vaccination. The most deadly factor about these vaccinations is that they seem so real. Then sincere people, thinking it is the real thing, pursue it with all their hearts.

As a pastor and counselor, I see this all the time. People come to church, then counseling, and they hear the Word of God. Yet they never really commit themselves to it or put it into practice. When things don't work, they say, "I tried God, but He didn't help." Actually, they didn't try God; they just got a vaccination. They did just enough of the real things and mixed them with just enough of the wrong things that it became a vaccine, keeping them from the real benefits.

These vaccinations contain mixed motives, which are very deadly. Some of the motives may be scriptural and genuine, but others are selfish. Because they're mixed, it is hard to tell which is which. In *The Message*, Proverbs 21:8 says, *"Mixed motives twist life into tangles; pure motives take you straight down the road."*

One of the most deadly vaccinations filled with mixed motives is the need to be needed. It is such a deep-seated and strong paradigm that few people will ever see their way past its deception. Being needed is one way to feel secure in a relationship. However, being needed is also the breeding ground for every form of codependency, deceit, and manipulation.

"I Need You"

Couples who do not love each other often stay together because they have needs. Since need is the motive for staying, there is little likelihood they will work out any of their problems. To confront the problems would threaten security and create the possibility that the need would not be met.

Codependency thrives in an environment of lack.[13] It was Satan who created the first sense of lack that lured Adam and Eve into his trap, and we've been falling into it ever since. When we feel lack, we can become desperate and shortsighted; we feel powerless to meet the needs that face us. Instead of depending on our relationship with God to meet those needs, we pull people into our environment and use them to meet those needs.

The need to be needed is prevalent in low self-worth. People with low self-worth don't believe anyone would want them for who they are or for the value of the relationship. They feel safe in relationships only when they are needed, so they look for people who will need them. As a result, they find themselves drawn to needy people, who usually cannot build a healthy relationship; so the cycle of rejection and codependency continues.

Love has value and respect for qualities it does not need. Need has value only for what meets the need.

If you or anyone else enters into a relationship based on need, that relationship will begin from a selfish, codependent perspective. Why? Need uses others to meet a need and values people solely on the basis of what they do for that need. Love, however, values people for who they are and has value and respect for qualities it does not need.

---

[13] For more on this topic, read *Escape from Codependent Christianity* (Huntsville, Alabama: Impact International Publications, 1997).

Brenda has many qualities that I respect but do not need. For instance, she has impeccable taste. In our travels across the country we often see something that is popular in another region. You can be sure that if she likes something, it may soon be popular nationwide. I have no need for that kind of taste. I have little interest in fashion. It does not add to the quality of my life, but I do respect this quality in Brenda. It adds to my esteem (*agape*) for her. On the other hand, a need-oriented person not only may have no value for whatever does not meet his or her need, but that person may also be threatened by it!

When the need-oriented person is attracted to someone, he or she sometimes tries to make the other person feel needy. To make someone else feel needy, you must either point out your strengths or point out the other person's weaknesses. Either way, it never works; it always fails to produce the desired effect. When people recognize they are in desperate need, they often question their love. They don't know if they love or need the other person, and sometimes they even despise the person they need. They feel trapped in the arrangement.

> It is not need that makes a relationship strong, but desire.

The greatest tragedy of the need-oriented arrangement is that it allows no room for personal growth. If either person grows, he or she won't need the other; personal growth might signal the end of the relationship.

Need versus Freedom

Our church is an incredible environment for building self-worth. Everything about our approach to ministry avoids codependency. We build a deep sense of Bible-based self-worth in people. We help them discover their new identity in Jesus. We see people make incredible strides, face issues, and live their dreams when they come to believe the truth about their identity in Jesus. Surprisingly, the main obstacle to growth that we encounter is a controlling mate who needs to be needed.[14]

Of all the things that threaten a need-oriented relationship, personal growth would be the greatest. Why? If you are with me because you need me, then anything that makes you not need me is a threat to the security of our relationship. People who need to be needed can easily shift into the control mode. In their minds it is a reasonable thing to do. They are filled with the mixed motives of love and need. They see their control as noble and loving. After all, if their spouses grow beyond their need, there is no longer any reason for the relationship. The unrealized goal of people who want to be needed becomes "to keep you from growing"—to keep you needy!

There are many ways—both conscious and unconscious—a person can maintain the need arrangement. One way is to accentuate a particular strength. This is a common tactic of the insecure. It looks like ego, but it is actually the epitome of insecurity: "I am so insecure that I will flaunt or exaggerate my strength instead of developing relationship skills." Sometimes this becomes the very thing that drives the other person away instead of making him or her stay. Their desperate search to find a strength that would cause someone to need the person can eventually become an obsession.

Bob came to me because he felt that Mary was pulling away from him. When they married, he believed that

---

[14] There are many other reasons for a spouse to be controlling. In this context, control emerges when one spouse begins to grow.

he would make the relationship secure by providing a financially secure life. Anytime there was discontentment in the marriage, Bob would do something to add to his image as a financial provider.

When Mary would try to talk to him about her feelings of loneliness, he felt like a failure. He kept trying to make her see that she had no reason to be unhappy. After all, the bills were paid and they lived in a nice house in a safe neighborhood. What more could anyone want? Mary's discontentment grew.

As Bob began to put an overemphasis on financial provision, Mary lost hope that he would ever "get the picture." His continual emphasis on money caused her to despise him. They came in for counseling at the point of divorce.

Bob had gotten "a vaccination" when he was young. Since his parents went through financially difficult times that ultimately led to a divorce, he saw the need to be a great provider. That was a reality. But he mixed this reality with his fear of intimacy, and it became a vaccine instead of a vitamin. It kept him from the marital security for which he deeply longed.

When you seek to fill your need for security through needy people, your life will be a cycle of failed relationships. For much of my life I was driven by insecurity. I always found women who needed me, but then I despised them because they had no personal identity or purpose. Their only purpose was to find security through me. It was a horrible cycle of attraction and rejection. Meeting the needs in the lives of the women I dated was a vaccine. It looked like love, but it wasn't. Still, I stayed in relationships where I could not experience the real thing.

One of my greatest attractions to Brenda was the fact that she challenged me. She was not someone who would just "lie down and take it." She was the first strong woman I ever got close to. I knew I needed someone with strength.

Although Brenda was strong in many areas, she still wanted me to need her. I was willing to be interdependent, but not codependent. By then I had recognized the need for genuine love—something we all need. But I also knew I didn't need love through a specific person; I could live without her if I had to. Too often we tend to confuse our real needs with the person through whom those needs are met.

We tend to confuse our real needs with the person through whom those needs are met.

My refusal to need her was very threatening for Brenda, and we had many arguments over this issue. It took years for her to realize that it is not need, but desire, that would make our relationship strong. We didn't want to despise, yet need, one another. We wanted to be together because there was desire, passion, and value. Today Brenda joyfully tells people that the greatest day in her life was the day she realized she didn't need me.

Freedom and responsibility always come in equal measure. To the degree that you experience freedom, you must equally accept responsibility. That's how we are freed from the game-playing and manipulation. But with freedom, we are faced with incredible responsibility. In other words, if I want Brenda to value me, I must be valuable. If I want her to desire me, I must be desirable. If I want her to have passion for me, I must stir that passion in her. This type of relationship demands that we put forth effort. We must continue to develop ourselves as interesting, desirable people.

I Need to Be Needed

Is yours a relationship built on love or an arrangement built on need? Do you make yourself desirable to your mate? What do you do to keep yourself interesting and romantic? Do you try to make your mate realize his or her need for you? Do you overemphasize strengths to make your mate need you? Do you make your mate feel needed or appreciated? Begin today to make the changes necessary to break the cycle.

Chapter 16

Safe Communication

Chapter 16

Safe Communication

Making a person feel safe in intimacy starts with communication. If your spouse doesn't feel safe talking to you, he or she will never feel safe in intimacy. Passionate love flourishes in openness and honesty, but it withers in the drought of communication. If you wait until you get to the bedroom to earn trust, you're too late. Rather, the bedroom is the place you want to go where you never have a concern or fear about what is going to happen.

We talked about communication briefly in some earlier chapters, but let's look at it in some more depth here.

It's All about Value

Communication is the fertile ground from which every form of love grows. The number one complaint from most wives is about communication. "My husband doesn't talk to me." This happens so much that it has been erroneously assumed that the desire to communicate is a solely feminine characteristic. As a result, some men resist sharing their thoughts and feelings for fear that it will make them appear weak.

Contrary to popular belief, communication is not exclusively feminine. Men actually talk as much as women. However, a few decades ago when women mostly stayed at home during the day, men often complained about their wives' need for communication. The difference was that most men talked all day at work and were emotionally and physically tired when they came home, but the wife had no meaningful communication all day, while the husband was at work. So when he came home from work, she was ready to talk while he was ready for quiet. Much of that has changed in today's world, but the stereotype is still very much alive.

The truth is that the desire to talk is a behavioral tendency, not a gender issue. There are men who love to talk and there are women who love to talk. The fact that a man wants to talk does not mean he is weak. It is not a deflowering of his masculinity. The most powerful men in the world are those who know how to communicate and negotiate. Every day the heads of countries sit down with other leaders and discuss delicate issues that will alter the course of our world. Many businessmen daily negotiate multimillion-dollar deals that create our national economy.

So the real issue about communication is not a "male-female" issue; it is a values issue. We talk to people whom we value about things that we value: We transact business deals; we broker loans; we answer questions for customers. Why? We value the paycheck. That value gives us the emotional resources we need to communicate. Then when we come home, we expect our mates to do all that we want out of obligation. We want the emotional payday, and we certainly want the passionate payday. But are we as willing to invest in our relationships as we are in our jobs?

What does that mean, you ask? Let me put it this way: Are you interested in your mate's life? Do you want to know about his or her day? Are you interested in what your spouse has experienced and accomplished? Are his or her feelings really important? Is your mate precious enough that you care about his or her life? Communication is a signpost along the road to affection and passion. If you don't see one, you are lost and traveling down the wrong path.

In some counseling sessions, people often reveal the idea that if they had a great sex life, all the other areas of their lives would be great. I personally have never seen it work that way. I have seen couples who had only a sex life. That's all that was left of their marriage. But I have never seen good sex save a marriage over the long haul. Think about it. Would that satisfy you?

Communication is a signpost along the road to affection and passion. If you don't see one, you are lost and traveling down the wrong path.

No, what we really want is a great relationship. We want to feel loved. We want dignity and worth. We want our mates to have value for us in every area of life, not just the bedroom. The truth is that a great sex life is the product of a great relationship. Great relationships produce great sex! And great relationships are built through great communication.

Betty came to me for counseling. She really loved her husband and wanted a happy marriage. He wanted the marriage to work, too, but he didn't understand what it would take. He thought that if they had great sex, all their other problems would be resolved. They wanted the same thing, but like so many couples today their communication was so poor, they couldn't find the route that would cause them to arrive at the same destination.

One day after the counseling session had formally ended, Betty and I talked a little about her personal dreams. I didn't say very much; I just let her talk while I listened. From time to time I encouraged her and assured her that she could fulfill her life's dreams. At the end of the conversation she thanked me for listening and said, "What we just shared was better than sex. If only my husband could understand my need for communication."

What she ultimately communicated was the fact that she would want to have sex with her husband more if he showed value and interest in her life, especially when it came to communication. Too often people pay attention only when they want something. It is a *Conversation is the best form of foreplay in the world.* terrible turnoff to our mates if we are attentive and affectionate only when we want sex. That is nothing more than self-seeking manipulation. It robs our mate of any sense of value and dignity.

Communication and Respect

Conversation is the best form of foreplay in the world. In fact, listening when other people speak is one of the most powerful ways to communicate value (*agape*). I am not always interested in the things that my wife is interested in, but I am always interested in her. When she talks, I listen, and she repays the kindness. We show mutual respect for one another's interests because we have mutual respect for each other.

Some years ago I came to this realization: "When you let other people do all the talking, they think you are the most interesting person in the world." Now, Brenda and I have totally different interests. We are so different in so many areas. I am active in several outdoor sports; she works on the inside of the house. I teach and preach; she nurtures the children and grandchildren. I can live anywhere; she likes things tasteful and beautiful. But we also have things for which we share a common value: We have children whom we love, we have dreams, and we both want to walk with God. I don't always know what to say, but I always know how to listen.

When Brenda talks about things that are of no interest to me, I look her in the eyes and remind myself how much I love her. I try to really look at her and remember all that I value about her. I listen to her because I believe this is the respect she deserves. My value for her empowers me to show interest in her, even when I am not interested in what she is talking about.

Ted and Sarah were at the point of divorce because they felt they didn't have enough in common. They felt their lives were going in different directions, and they were. However, they had been taught that a man and wife should have the same dreams. Ted wanted to be a pastor. Sarah had no interest in fitting into the role of a pastor's wife. She didn't sing, teach, or play piano. They thought their marriage was over.

Fortunately, Brenda models complete freedom as a pastor's wife. She does not fit the stereotype and has no intention or need to do so. We shared with this couple how we both had our own lives and our own passionate interests, but that they had never pulled us apart. There are two things that pull a couple apart when they have different interests. The first is one partner's attempt to force the other to have the same interests. The second is one partner's lack of communication and interest in the things his or her mate has an interest in. Brenda and I share our different lives with one another with the confidence that the other one cares and is interested.

One of our household rules is this: "If it is important to you, it is important." This is how God responds to us. We can pray about anything, and He is always there. He always cares. He is always ready to respond and help us in any situation. Because we've established this rule in our marriage, we are able to talk about anything without fear of looking or sounding foolish.

Another important rule we have is, "Show respect." Early in our marriage we made a pact to never kid or joke in a way that could damage the other's self-worth. We never make fun of each other. We never say what we don't mean either in jest or in anger.

Proverbs warns about saying damaging things and then saying, "Oh, I was just kidding."[15] Whether you mean it or not, the damage is done. This Scripture goes on to explain how these words go into us and do damage. I see couples joke about their mates being overweight, make cutting remarks about the other's cooking, or criticize the other's talents. They might not realize it, but those words become seeds that grow into a harvest of insult and diminished self-worth. What's worse is what you say in anger. If you don't mean it, don't say it.

By protecting our communication in this manner Brenda and I have protected our self-worth. We have kept the level of esteem high. We have made it safe to say anything, even "No!"

---

[15] Proverbs 26:18–19 says, "*Like a madman shooting firebrands or deadly arrows is a man who deceives his neighbor and says, 'I was only joking!'*" (NIV).

What kind of relationship do you want? Some good questions for you to consider are these: "Do I listen when my mate talks? Do I look at my spouse so he or she knows I am interested in him or her? Do I say things I don't really mean when I am angry or just kidding?" Ask your mate to tell you at least one thing that you do when you kid or when you are angry that he or she does not appreciate. Show your love by apologizing and make a commitment to never introduce that hurt into your relationship again.

Chapter 17

Who's the Boss?

Chapter 17

Who's the Boss?

In Ephesians 5:31 Paul said these eternal words: *"And the two shall become one"* (NKJV). The unanswered question is, which one? From the moment that serious dating evolves, the struggle begins to see who's going to actually be boss. Who's going to be in charge? Which one will the couple become?

Brenda and I are both very strong-willed, independent people. Our marriage could have been a matrimonial clash of the Titans. We both had very strong opinions about how things should be done. And we were both willing to stand up for those opinions. Our views on child-raising, money management, health issues, and communication, just to name a few, were completely different.

When I was younger, I was very confrontational with our kids. I didn't negotiate. She was more relaxed and conversational. Both of our styles had strengths, but they also had weaknesses. When it came to managing money, I would pay the bills even if I didn't have food to eat. Brenda would say, "Take care of the needs of the family, then pay the bills." On these and other issues we both had valid, positive points, but the question was, who was going to win? Who was really the boss?

In many areas we struggled through the same kind of issues as everyone else does. We both tried to force our views on the other. But as we talked about what we wanted, it became obvious that we both wanted the same thing. We wanted happy, well-adjusted children. We wanted to be free from the struggles of financial lack. We wanted to be healthy. In almost every area we were struggling for the same thing. So who was right?

As in all areas of life, no one person is completely right and no one is completely wrong. My respect for her made me listen and consider what she had to say. However, for me there was a scriptural paradigm that had to be corrected before I could benefit from her insight.

I came from a background that said women should submit to men. Although I had never seen that Scripture work in practical, daily situations, I had enough male chauvinism in me to attempt to use it to my advantage. At the same time, my conscience would not let me use force as a way to win the battle for control. And that was part of the problem. I found that sometimes when I argued or stood up for something, it was more about being right or being in control than it was about solving the issues.

Bossing versus Yielding

As I prayerfully reviewed the Scriptures on relationship, I saw what had eluded me for years. Before the Bible ever said, *"Wives, submit to your own husbands,"* it first said, *"Giving thanks always for all things to God the Father in the name of our Lord Jesus Christ, submitting to one another in the fear of God"* (Ephesians 5:20–22 NKJV). This Scripture did not fit into the mind-set that I had accepted for the biblical model of husband and wife. This did not even compute with my erroneous definition of submission!

You see, submission is not obedience. It is an attitude of yielding. In successful marriages, both parties should be thankful for one another and have a yielding attitude toward each other. "That's nice," you may say, "but this still does not answer the question of who gets to be boss." If you're still asking that question, you are still missing the point. In a biblically-based marriage neither one gets to boss the other.

Submission is not obedience. It is an attitude that is yielding.

If Jesus is Lord in our lives, then we should have a desire and a commitment to see what His Word says about every issue. So the highest commitment should not be to determine *who* is right, but to find out *what* is right. What is the truth and how should it be applied to this particular problem? This is the question asked by the wise in heart.

If both parties are yielded to one another, both are open to the other's point of view. Eventually Brenda and I reached a place where we didn't care who was right. We just wanted one of us to find the answers. It didn't matter which one.

We found that we both had good ideas, but our ideas had to be tempered to work in our situation. For example, when our children were certain ages, she was much better with them than I was. At other ages and in different issues, I was much more effective.

We faced our greatest struggle, however, when it came to money issues. She went for quality, while I went for "just get by." She was constantly stretching me to think "quality."

I wanted quality, but quality cost more. Or so I thought! As we look back, she was definitely over the top on financial issues while I was in the basement. I would have never become financially independent without her influence, yet she never would have been able to save a dime without my influence.

As we worked through these things, the two of us became one new person because we were both yielded to one another. Together we have both become someone we weren't. I like who I have become by listening to and yielding to my wife. It has freed me from the burden of needing to be right all the time. It gave me relief from making every decision alone. I didn't have to solve all the problems. I had a teammate, one who was helping me become a new man with a new point of view. And she was becoming a new woman with a new point of view. Today we are not the people we were. And we got where we are because we became a team. We helped shape each other's life.

In a biblically based marriage, neither one gets to boss the other.

Teamwork Creates Oneness

Today when I see marriages fraught with control issues, I am saddened. I know that I am witnessing two people who will never become who they could be in marriage, in relationship, and in God because they don't view the other person as a team member.

I was surprised when looking at recent divorce statistics. It seemed as though the divorce rate for fundamental Christians was just slightly higher than it was for non-Christians. Based on my counseling experience, I couldn't help but think that male chauvinistic interpretations of the Scriptures might play a role in this problem.

It seems that men have a tendency to take a few Scriptures out of context, ignore foundational principles, and justify control and sometimes abuse. (Women sometimes use those same Scriptures as a way to escape personal responsibility.) I have attended marriage seminars by renowned "family teachers" who created a male supremacy paradigm that cripples any opportunity for real love and relationship. All it takes is the abandonment of a few principles for Scripture to be twisted into anything we want it to say.

When women feel they are in a male chauvinistic environment, they become closed and resistant to their mates. They feel forced to accept the view of their husbands. It was, after all, male chauvinism that fueled a reactionary women's liberation movement. Many women are tired of living in what is viewed as "a man's world." Since they don't have the backing of the church to gain their freedom, they are forced to resort to more subtle control tactics like withholding sex and other manipulation tactics. In the end it doesn't matter who is having a problem; the results are the same.

We must remember that *agape*-love that has value, holds the other as precious, and maintains esteem must undergird every scriptural application. When it is not applied in love (*agape*), truth is no longer true. We also must realize that we are never allowed to use force or domination to impose our scriptural perspectives.

If a man desires to accept his role as head of the family, he must realize that the head is the one who accepts responsibility. In other words, we men should be the ones who make sure that these principles are observed in the relationship. After all, the Scriptures do point to the man as the one who should initiate love (*agape*) in the relationship. *"Husbands, love your wives, just as Christ also loved the church and gave Himself for her"* (Ephesians 5:25 NKJV).

Love accepts the responsibilities of the role and never claims the privileges. Jesus never demanded that the world see or accept Him as Lord. He offered the truth in love and allowed people to make their own choices. His love compelled us to love and trust Him. Through His relationship to mankind, He became the model for how a man should relate to his wife—He never used force or coercion.

Sexual compliance, on the other hand, is all too often an act of "scriptural" coercion. First Corinthians 7:4 says, *"The wife hath not power of her own body, but the husband: and likewise also the husband hath not power of his own body, but the wife."* For many this verse has become the "proof text" for sex on demand. I disagree. When you read it in context, this passage is talking about people who stop having sex in order to focus on seeking God. They are encouraged to do so only by agreement. This is not a general teaching about sexual obligation.

In verse 6 Paul pointed out, *"But I say this as a concession, not as a commandment"* (NKJV). This is not a commandment. This is not something he received from the Lord for instruction in marriage. He said this as a concession to those who struggle with sexual desire.

The moment we use obligation as the tool to get a person to act, the emotional quality of the response degenerates. We will not experience the passion and affection we desire. When a man or woman determines to be boss in this area, he or she will introduce fear and insecurity into intimacy. It is important to realize that foreplay for the next sexual encounter begins with this sexual encounter. We can make our mates look forward to the next time or dread it based on how we handle it this time.

The Message does such a great job of clarifying these passages about sexual fulfillment.

> *Sexual drives are strong, but marriage is strong enough to contain them and provide for a balanced and fulfilling sexual life in a world of sexual disorder. The marriage bed must be a place of mutuality — the husband seeking to satisfy his wife, the wife seeking to satisfy her husband. Marriage is not a place to "stand up for your rights." Marriage is a decision to serve the other, whether in bed or out.*
>
> (1 Corinthians 7:3–5)

Without the mutual input of both team members, you can never become the new person that God intends you to be.

Using Scripture to make things go your way causes your mate to despise both you and God. The moment you use a Scripture to get someone to violate his or her will, you have gone beyond the scope of the Word of God. You are attempting to bend the other person to your will. And what's worse is you are willing to pervert that person's view of God to do so.

No matter if it is about the bedroom, raising kids, managing finances, or buying a car, when either you or your spouse tries to be boss, you are no longer able to function as a team. You have lost one-half of who you are. If you are not functioning as a team, there will automatically be a struggle for power. In the end someone will feel like he or she is not valuable and needed. Ultimately, without the mutual input of both team members, you can never become the new person God intends you to be. Nothing has influenced my life as much as yielding to my wife. I know she feels the same way. The day I turned in my boss's badge and got a team uniform, everything changed for the better.

The next time you demand your rights, just remember it will not come out the way you want it to, even if you get what you want. Wouldn't you rather have a lifetime of fulfillment than a moment of forced pleasure?

Do you view your spouse as a teammate? Ask your spouse if he or she feels like a part of a team or an employee working for someone else. Are you more concerned about who is right or what is right? Ask your mate, "Do we make decisions together? Do you feel like we both have equal input and equal responsibility in the decisions that affect our family?" Are you just as happy when your mate finds the solution as you are when you find the solution? Are you growing together to become a new person, or are you trying to change your spouse to be like you?

Chapter 18

It's All in Your Mind

Chapter 18

It's All in Your Mind

Sex is about ninety percent mental and ten percent physical. The pleasure derived from sex is more about what happens emotionally than what takes place physically. Those who experience only physical gratification are never truly fulfilled. Some give up the hope that sexual intimacy can ever be an exceptional experience. Others begin a constant search for the illusive sexual experience—the experience that they *imagine* they should be having.

Believe it or not, imagination is the fuel of life. It all goes back to the fact that God told us to love Him with all our hearts, souls, and minds. (See Mark 12:30.) That word for *mind* includes the concept of imagination and deep meditative thoughts. Thus the degree we involve our imagination in any experience increases the emotional impact of that experience.

You see the power of imagination in a negative way in the pornography industry. The power of pornography is rooted completely in the imagination. People watch pornography and imagine a sexual experience that is beyond anything they will ever physically experience. And the road people take to sexual abuse is often their search for an experience that is as powerful as their imagination.

On the other hand, if we used this type of imagination in a positive way, our sexual intimacy with our mates would have the potential to bond us to them for life. We could have incredible levels of openness and intimacy. This can only happen, however, when there is complete freedom from the fear of abuse, misuse, criticism, or embarrassment. Safe sex is sex that takes place when both parties feel completely safe.

Make Your Mind Work for You

I have used my imagination to keep my love life alive and vibrant for years. That may surprise you, but let me explain how it works. In the Old Testament, God taught the children of Israel to create associations. He would tell them to put a stack of rocks in a certain place. Then, when their children would ask about those rocks, the parents were to tell them some incredible story about God's deliverance. They would do the same thing by writing Scriptures on the wall and with many of the other ornamental things that are part of the Jewish culture. Eventually, when you would look at those rocks, those Scriptures, or those symbols, you would remember and automatically experience something in your heart with God. I realized that I could use this same power of remembrance to create great associations with my wife.

I had a photo of Brenda that I really liked. It was taken around the time I first began to notice her and develop strong feelings for her. I would often look at that photo and remember all the things that attracted me to her. I would think of all the things I loved about her. I used this to create what some people call a trigger. By creating this emotional trigger, I could rekindle all those feelings anytime I looked at that photo. It was like having a button to push when I wanted to be "in love" again.

In time it developed to a place where I could recall that image in my mind and immediately remember and experience all those feelings of love and passion that I had for her in the beginning. That meant I could feel as in love twenty years later as I did the first day. Why did I do this? I wanted to have a level of intimacy that keeps me passionate for my wife. I wanted to have the ability to connect emotionally every time we touched or looked at one another. I don't want to have a day where the fire is not burning hot!

What people have failed to recognize about sexual fulfillment is that it is almost "all in our mind." The degree of physical gratification we experience is based more on what we are thinking when we make love than anything else. We can have the same wonderful sexual experiences today that we had when our love was new. But that can happen only if we keep our hearts alive with all those same thoughts and feelings.

For years we have had a clinic as a part of our ministry. We major on substance abuse, pain management, and eating disorders. In the past, however, we treated all types of health disorders. We have had numerous men and women experiencing various levels of impotency and lowered sex drive. Although there are often some physical problems, almost always the issue must be resolved in their thoughts and beliefs. Even after we have corrected a physical problem, people must deal with their fears about sexual failure. When people's minds are preoccupied with any kind of negative emotion, the ability to perform and the capacity to experience are diminished.

The man who is afraid he will not be able to perform adequately will live out his fear. The woman who has a dread of sexual intimacy will not have a good experience.

If we take stress or unresolved conflict into our bedrooms, it will rob us of a positive experience. Tom and Liz were in that very situation. Preoccupation with fears and uncertainties was robbing them of the freedom to give themselves to one another freely. Tom had been very sexually active as a young man, but Liz had a more wholesome background.

Liz was always bothered by the fact that her husband was more experienced than she was. Their honeymoon was a little awkward for her. Rather than the two of them growing in sexual discovery together, she felt like a "child" with an experienced man. In her mind she made unfair judgments about herself. She assumed that he could not enjoy sex with her compared to the "wild women" of his past.

Sexual intimacy is a physical activity where two people connect emotionally.

Nothing was further from the truth. He respected her for her wholesome past. It had never crossed his mind to compare her to anyone. He felt very special and loved. She felt very threatened and insecure. It took a lot of healthy communication and reassurances to overcome what was happening in her mind so that she could be free to experience the intimacy of the moment. She had to create new associations with sexual intimacy. She had to stop thinking the old destructive thoughts and put on new positive beliefs.

How to Keep the Flame Alive

If you will take these steps to create loving associations, you will always have good, intimate experiences. First, you need to know every reason you love your mate. You need to be aware of and thankful for every positive thing he or she brings to your life. When you hold him or her in your arms, you need to be experiencing more than a physical moment. You need to be experiencing everything you value, everything that is precious about your mate.

Whether my wife and I are making love or holding hands, I can experience all the passion and emotions of our love. It is simply a matter of stirring up my memories. Again, it is not your mate's physical beauty or his or her sexual prowess that makes intimacy wonderful. The power of your sexual experience is all in your mind. It is about value, preciousness, and esteem. It is about the associations that you create for intimacy.

One of the things I do to keep my passions alive is what I call capturing moments. There are those moments when Brenda does or says something or smiles a certain way. For some reason, an expression or word touches my heart. When I notice that something is influencing my emotions, I attempt to capture it in my visual memory. Then when I recall that visual picture, I experience that moment again. I now have such a catalog of captured moments that I can recall and reexperience almost any positive emotion I desire.

People use these skills by default every day. It is just this type of capturing moments that causes them to become consumed with lust for someone other than their spouses. This does not make these skills evil; it just means that people tend to use them more for evil than for good.

I have a simple thing I do nearly every time I am in morning prayer. I create a visual image of my wife. I see her in the most compelling way. Then I silently remind myself that we are one. I create a mental image of us stepping into one another and then together stepping into Jesus. It is as if we are huddled together and you can't tell where one starts and the other stops. I thank God for my wife. I renew my commitment to walk in love that day. I spend a few minutes considering how it feels to be that connected to one another in Jesus. Just that simple exercise is one of the greatest immunities I have ever found to adulterous thoughts.

By making intimacy all about an emotional connection, Brenda and I have always had a good sex life. Sexual intimacy is a physical activity where we connect emotionally. And it is the emotional connection that makes it great. The physical aspect is secondary.

What do you remember about your mate that caused you to desire him or her? Make a list. What do you notice today that makes your mate desirable? The next time you touch, think about all that you value in your mate. Notice the difference in what you experience. Take some time to rekindle your first passions. Find a photo of your spouse that was taken at a time when your desire was the strongest. Get in touch with all those feelings again. Learn to call them back at will. Take steps in your prayer time to create a sense of being one. Make it a point never to have another purely physical moment with your mate. Always draw upon all that you value and cherish about him or her.

Chapter 19

A Lifetime of Great Lovemaking

Chapter 19

A Lifetime of Great Lovemaking

While on a business trip, I was accompanied by a young man who had been married for only a few weeks. Several times throughout the day he would mention his wife. He often spoke of missing her. I noticed that when these emotions were stirred, they were usually sexually related. Now, this is not uncommon or unhealthy for a newlywed. After all, sexual relations are meant to be so powerful that they physically bond us to one person for life.

One night during dinner he frantically jumped up, looked at his watch, and exclaimed, "I forgot to call my wife!" After he left the table, another associate mentioned that he had done that nearly every day while on the trip.

The thought came to my mind, *How sad it is that he thinks of her and misses her sexually, but he doesn't think of her when it comes to conversation.* This is probably the experience of many young men. And, sadly, this is a forecast of the types of issues this young man's marriage will probably one day face.

I never wanted to get a cell phone; I already had limited privacy. I pastor a growing church; we have a fellowship of ministers, a Bible college, and various outreaches; and I am involved in a few business ventures. As I like to use "drive time" for deep thought and serenity, I dreaded the idea that I could always be found. The thing that finally compelled me to take the plunge was the desire to talk to my wife when I was away from home. For years Brenda traveled with me as much as possible. When our grandchildren began to arrive, she stopped traveling with me as much as before. She wanted to be there to help our children through the difficult time of adjustment. But I still wanted to talk to her.

When I am away, we may talk as often as five times a day. She is the person I want to share my life with. I want her to know my thoughts, fears, ideas, and dreams. I enjoy just hearing her voice. Because I travel so much, the telephone became an important tool in developing our communication skills.

> Sex starts with the last time you made love. And intimacy tonight starts at breakfast this morning.

Love Listens

In those telephone calls I found that conversation is the best foreplay possible. However, you must remember that sexual stimulation also started the last time you made love. And intimacy tonight starts at breakfast this morning. I believe that foreplay is the conversation that takes place between spouses during the day. You see, intimacy *starts* when we have emotional and physical connection. It is always a process. So a day that ends in passionate intimacy is usually a day that starts with warmth and affection. If you wait until you are "in the mood" to talk, it might be too late. I have found that a lifetime of great sex is the product of a great relationship, a great friendship.

Some people complain, "I don't know what he or she wants. I don't know how to make my mate happy."[16] If you really communicated, you would always know what the other person wants and needs. You have to learn to be an effective listener. Studies reveal that different people listen for different things. Some people only listen to gather information about their interests; some listen to evaluate, some to comprehend. "It is estimated that people screen out or misunderstand the intended meaning, or purpose, of what they hear in over 70 percent of all communications."[17] Sadly, you hear what you are listening for and little else.

When I decided that I wanted to make people feel loved, I realized that few people would actually come out and tell me much of what I needed to know. As often as not, when people do try to tell someone something, they sometimes don't really get it right. Proverbs describes a wise person as one who can draw counsel out of another person.[18] A listener asks questions, in a non-threatening way, and gathers information until he or she understands.

Love doesn't look to its own needs only. It considers the good of others. You can discover what people value when you listen to them. People reveal what they value when they tell stories. When you see a person's face light up, you know something is special to him or her. When you get into a conversation with someone that could go on forever, you have found that person's point of interest. When something makes people laugh or cry, you have found what touches their hearts. Nothing says "I love you"

[16] Keep in mind that it really isn't possible for you to make someone happy if that person has not developed the capacity for personal happiness.
[17] Personal Listening Profile, Inscape Publishing (formerly Carlson Learning Company), Minneapolis, Minnesota, 1995.
[18] Proverbs 20:5 says, "Counsel in the heart of man is like deep water; but a man of understanding will draw it out."

as much as discovering something important to a person without him or her having to tell you.

At this point you may be wondering, "But what does this have to do with sex?" Well, it has little to do with sex, but it has everything to do with romantic, affectionate, intimate lovemaking! This is the "life of foreplay" that brings you to a lifetime of sexually intimate gratification.

The time and effort you put into effective listening will be what develops your skills at intimacy. Relatively few people know how to be intimate. Intimacy is not a gift; it is a skill. And skills don't come automatically; they are developed through learning and practice. The opposite of being intimate is being distant. Being intimate is being close—physically, emotionally, and heart-close.

A lifetime of great sex is the product of a great life together.

Love Exercises Self-Control

As I mentioned earlier, when people feel safe in communication, it opens the door to all other levels of intimacy. If you can trust me on this level of emotional vulnerability, you will risk deeper levels. I can't over-emphasize that you must make your mate feel safe if you want love to flourish on all levels.

Self-control is highly respected and a breeding ground for feelings of safety. People who control themselves verbally usually have more control over other parts of their lives and anatomy.[19] People who control their tongues when their passions are enraged will probably control their sexual urges when necessary. Always be able to stop sexual

[19] See James 3:1–2.

stimulations when signs indicate that your mate is not enjoying the endeavor. If you want the ultimate trust, self-control will make it happen.

Never go where you do not have permission to go. Jesus modeled perfect love when He obtained the keys to the kingdom of God, yet presented all of it to the Father. (See 1 Corinthians 15:24.) Philippians 2 tells us that He did not consider His rights as Lord something to be clung to; therefore, He emptied Himself and became a man. Perfect love never claims rights. As servants of God we are truly qualified only when we realize we are free from obligation. Then love compels us to do what we are no longer obligated by the law to do. As believers we are motivated by love, not rights. Love never forces its way. It always waits for permission.

True love says, "You have given me your life; now I give it back to you."

Even though the Scriptures say that our bodies belong to our mates, the person of love never claims that as a right. True love says, "You have given me your life; now I give it back to you. I only want from you what you willingly and joyfully give." This is the attitude that breeds a lifetime of great lovemaking.

The incredible perks you get from this type of life are beyond description in this book. There is not an area of life where you will not realize the benefits. Being a better husband has made me a better father, a better boss, a better pastor, and a better friend. My business skills have grown enormously. My capacity to negotiate and create wealth has developed beyond anything I ever imagined. And I have a completely new dimension for experiencing God's love. Anything that is truly "spiritual" and scripturally consistent always affects every area of your life. Being intimate with your mate affects your capacity for intimacy with God, and vice versa.

Do you know what you listen for? Does your mate often say that you don't listen? What communication skills do you need to learn? On a scale of one to ten, how much verbal self-control do you have? On the same scale, how would you rate yourself with sexual control? Can you stop without inflicting guilt or projecting anger on your mate? What do the stories your mate tells indicate that he or she values? What do you know about your mate based on his or her communication? How could you use this knowledge to make your spouse feel loved? What steps can you take today to make yourself a better listener?

Chapter 20

Feeling Loved

Chapter 20

Feeling Loved

Everyone wants to feel love. It is the deepest need of a human being. This need is inherent because we were created to be God's family, and He gave us this unique capacity to experience His love. This sets us apart from all other created beings. Even the angels lack this capacity. This was the highest purpose for our creation: to live in loving harmony and relationship with God as our Father. This is why we were created.

Every positive human emotion grows from our capacity to experience love. On the other hand, every negative human emotion grows from our feelings of fear. All emotions are determined by these two opposing emotional factors. Emotionally healthy people feel loved. Dysfunctional emotions and unacceptable behavior evolve from the absence of love and the subsequent distorted attempts to find love beyond the scope of God's defined realities.

Probably the number one issue that emerges in any counseling session is a person's inability to give and receive love. In simple language, rejection. Rejection is an emotional sense that may not be based on reality. It is, however, the reality experienced by the person who has not developed the capacity to experience true love.

The rejected person does not have the ability to give and receive love.

The Rejection Syndrome

Although everyone has the potential to feel love, not everyone has, at this moment, the capacity. Deep within all of us is the vague, sometimes undefined desire for love. But our beliefs about ourselves, love, and God limit our capacity to experience love.

The inability to experience love is based on past experiences and current associations. One example would be the girl who was molested as a child. Since her offender said he was doing it because he loved her, she developed a belief that love is expressed through sex. As a result, she lives an immoral life that destroys all self-worth. It twists her emotions. She despises herself and her immoral behavior, yet the need to feel loved drives her in this dysfunctional attempt to find love through sex. Because of her past beliefs and associations, she believes sex and love are one and the same.

Then there is the person who was physically abused as a child or witnessed physical abuse as a child. This person was told that the abuse was the product of love. As a result, that person will grow up with one of two extreme tendencies. A woman may feel that she has to be abused to experience love. The search for love could drive her to an abusive husband or to a life of masochistic tendencies.

The other extreme of the abused person would be to avoid love altogether, to be frightened by the possibility. After all, love is pain. She wants love, but she fears the pain. That woman may spend her entire life running from true love. The association is that love is pain, and she doesn't want to hurt anymore.

If the person is a male who witnessed the abuse of his mother, he may physically abuse all the women he "loves." This may drive women away from him, making love impossible. Or it may attract women who associate pain and love, which still makes love impossible.

Although these are extreme examples, the truth is that the average person has very little capacity to experience real love. Most of what people associate with love is not at all like the love God has for us. Subsequently, people spend their entire lives seeking what they believe is love and never finding satisfaction. Such is the pursuit of the overly indulgent, the abuser, and occasionally the molester.

The rejected person, on the other hand, does not believe he or she is lovable. These individuals do not trust the love that people offer. They see it as threatening or disingenuous. People who expressed love in the past hurt or disappointed them; thus, their associations with love are not pleasant. They expect it to have a bad conclusion. They push love away, and they often respond in hostility when it is offered.

If you realize that you fit into one of these categories, you need to refer to chapter 4, "What's Love Got to Do with It?" and chapter 5, "You Can't Give What You Don't Have." You are looking for love, but you need to find its source first. Your search will find its end when you experience God's love. You will find personal freedom and the grace (God's ability) to love as you commit yourself to believing and showing God's love to the people in your world.

If you find yourself in a relationship with a person who lives in the rejection syndrome, you are no doubt discouraged, frustrated, and possibly enraged. You are living in an emotional vacuum. It seems that nothing you do is working. When you give too much, you find that the person takes more and is probably unappreciative. When you don't give enough, you are met with a barrage of unreasonable, illogical emotional responses. Your reaction, in the other person's mind, proves that his or her unrealistic imaginations are true and justifies his or her unreasonable responses.

You may be in a relationship with a person who is at this moment incapable of giving and receiving love. This means your deepest needs are not being met and your efforts at generating love are seldom appreciated. If you are one who is living with a person in a rejection syndrome, you may feel abused both emotionally and sexually. You are the recipient of real rejection.

Rejection is a self-perpetuating state of mind based on a faulty belief system.

To adequately deal with a person in the rejection syndrome would require a completely different book, but let me offer you some hope: This problem is not incurable! Anyone who is willing to take the necessary steps can come out of the rejection syndrome and find the capacity for meaningful love. Rejection is a very real experience, usually based on very real happenings. But you must understand that rejection is a self-perpetuating state of mind based on a faulty belief system.

Rejected people develop a lifestyle that protected them in a dysfunctional environment. They learn to survive by not trusting. They protect their hearts by closing themselves off emotionally. Although that behavior is a normal and essential tactic in that environment, it has just the opposite effect in a normal healthy environment. You can't punish the people who love you because of what someone else did to you. Walking is normal on dry ground, but if you try to walk on water, you're either going to sink or swim. When you're in the water you've got to swim; likewise, when you are relating to "normal" people, you can't use the survival tactics that protected you in a dysfunctional setting.

Although morals are absolute, behavior is determined by environment. When I am involved with people who are less than honest, the Bible says I would be a fool to be completely open and to reveal all. However, it also says that secret love is no better than an open rebuke. In other words, when I am in an environment of people who want to have a meaningful relationship, I need to open up and express myself. Thus, rejected people must develop a new survival system that works in healthy relationships. Otherwise, they become offenders to the current generation. They perpetuate the pain by duplicating it for others.

Our beliefs about ourselves, about love, and about God limit our capacity to experience love.

Find the Fine Line

If you are in a relationship with someone in this syndrome, there are some essential things you must realize and some absolute steps you must take. Let me caution you, though: You must move forward only with the realization that there is no guarantee of success. At the same time, because these steps are taken from a motive of *agape*-love, they offer the only hope of real results. When you begin walking in *agape*-love toward the rejected person, the

situation will either get worse or better—and it usually happens somewhat quickly.

I have witnessed many divorces resulting from people relentlessly walking in love because of those who walk in abuse. The positive aspect is that regardless of the particular outcome, you can be whole and have a life. Most people in a rejected relationship learn to just leave things alone. Attempts at solving the problems are often met with hostility or pouting, or it may set off a barrage of extreme reactionary behavior. When you no longer allow rejected people to define your behavior, you upset the system that sustains their dysfunction. As you begin to walk in God's love, they can no longer push you into extreme reactions that justify their behavior. As a result, they are forced by the environment to face and own their issues.

The rejected person needs, but doubts, real love (*agape*). If you intend to walk this through with your spouse, *agape*-love must be your commitment. Your spouse's reaction will be at best unpredictable. He or she may push against you to prove this self-fulfilling prophecy that love is not genuine. Or your mate may react in anger. Whatever the reaction, you must stay true to your commitment.

The fine line that you must discover lies in the invisible border between love and enabling. The rejected person generally finds ways to push things back to the way they were without ever really accepting responsibility for his or her actions. The worst thing you can do is the rejected person's part. You cannot take the steps that that person needs to take.

Jerry came to me because Anita constantly stayed in conflict. He was frustrated that she had not grown beyond her relational dysfunction. He blamed her totally for the problem. As we talked, I discovered that he usually became the go-between when she was in conflict with someone. He often tried to insulate her from the consequences of her actions.

When asked why he always got involved in her conflict, he boldly declared, "I love her. I'm not going to let her be hurt by all this conflict." What Jerry failed to see was that he was enabling Anita's dysfunction. She never had to face the consequences of her actions. He always intervened. With him doing her part, she would never grow up.

Love is defined by God's Word; it cannot be defined by the dysfunctional person. Showing value and preciousness can never be confused with doing the other person's part. Love is not giving in to unreasonable or unrealistic demands. Very often someone will challenge, "If you love me, you'll do this for me." The truth is, if it violates the Word of God or assumes your responsibilities, love will keep me from doing it for you.

You must seek to understand all you can about codependency[20] and rejection. Understanding should never be an excuse but rather the basis for an effective strategy. Understanding it is not about you will remove much of the sting from the unacceptable behavior you encounter. It is about the other person and his or her unresolved issues. If understanding becomes a basis for excuses and justification, then you have transformed into an enabler. You are now a part of making the problem incurable.

Rejected people need to be lovingly moved into facing their problems. This automatically happens when you

[20] *Escape from Codependent Christianity* (Huntsville, Alabama: Impact International Publications, 1997) is essential reading for the person who finds him- or herself in any part of this syndrome. Many accepted concepts of Christianity unwittingly encourage and enable codependency.

free yourself from the cycle. When you stop making excuses and stop accepting your spouse's responsibilities and overreactions, your spouse has no one to face but him- or herself. The person must accept responsibility for how his or her behavior is affecting the marriage; he or she needs to take personal steps for recovery and, in most cases, should seek qualified help.

Someone once said, "Giving someone all your love is never an assurance that they'll love you back! Don't expect love in return, just wait for it to grow in their hearts. But if it doesn't, be content it grew in yours."[21] Likewise, walking in God's love is no guarantee that a person will respond properly. But it is a guarantee that you will protect your heart regardless of what happens. People who get caught in the rejection game usually don't survive emotionally. If they stay married they don't survive, and if they get a divorce they don't survive. People who guard their hearts by walking in love ensure that they will have a future regardless of the outcome of the current situation.

Are you in a rejected relationship? Are you aware of any codependent tendencies in yourself that attracted you to this person? Are you accepting your responsibilities or are you attempting to blame-shift? Have you committed yourself to walking in God's love? Have you owned your tendencies to enable? Are you justifying unacceptable, reactionary behavior by your spouse's behavior? Are you more interested in getting your mate whole or getting him or her to meet your needs?

For the person who struggles with rejection, the following questions might be more appropriate. Do you trust when people attempt to express love toward you? Do you

[21] "Aspects of Love," Author unknown.

want people to prove their love to you? Are you uncomfortable in committed relationships? Do you feel awkward expressing love? Are you afraid of not being liked? Do you believe that God loves you? Upon what do you base that belief?

Regardless of which side of the fence you find yourself sitting, the cure is a commitment to God's *agape*-love. It must be your goal to know it, believe it, and give it.

Chapter 21

Obsession or Love?

Chapter 21

Obsession or Love?

Romance never thrives in an environment of obsession. I'm sure your first thought, after reading that opening statement, raced to the obsessive stalker. There are varying degrees and manifestations of obsession, however. There is the person who smothers you with attention. This person often looks like a loving individual until you take a closer look. He or she seems so attentive, but that attention is more like "watching." It is a mask!

Then there is the closet-obsessive who never really lets you know how he or she feels. This person has enough social awareness to know that controlling, obsessive behavior would not be tolerated. Yet the individual is in a constant inward struggle. The closet-obsessive does many if not all of the right things. He or she looks like the ideal mate. Because this person can mask the obsessive feelings, the true motives are hard to detect and nearly impossible to prove. But the one who lives with the obsessive person knows that beneath the caring, attentive surface lurks a deadly poison that strangles and smothers every possibility of love and romance.

The Subtleties of Obsession

Obsessive people are motivated by fear, not love. They are emotional addicts who crave the next fix. The person about whom they obsess is the drug. If they can just somehow get this person to meet their needs, the obsession will be satisfied. The truth is, no amount of control will ever get anyone to meet the needs of the obsessed. Because of the duplicity of these people's actions, they never bring about the desired results. An obsessive person conveys unspoken things that generate contempt, fear, and sometimes hatred. Still, obsessive actions are justified because, after all, "I'm doing the right thing."

In counseling I sometimes have a wife who is expressing a need for more romance. Very often the husband replies, "Every time I put my arm around you, you pull away. How can I be more romantic?" As I observe these types of conflicts, I often see obsession instead of romance.

> A truly romantic person is always aware of his or her mate's response to every level of stimulus.

Obsessive people convey something very negative, even when they do the "right" things. They make people feel overwhelmed, smothered, or controlled. I have often noticed that obsessive people inappropriately cling to their mates. They keep their arms around them a little too much. Or they want to hold hands when it is awkward. For them, physical contact is more about security or control than love. Inwardly they are afraid of losing their mates; outwardly this is expressed through socially acceptable control. Their actions convey anything but romance. They send signals of insecurity, not trust.

Remember, a truly romantic person is always aware of his or her mate's response to every level of stimulus. If it is for your spouse, you make sure your spouse enjoys it. When it is for you, you make your mate feel obligated. The moment you realize that your actions are not enjoyable or pleasant for the other person, stop what you are doing. Show your spouse that you value his or her feelings.

Brenda was incredibly challenging to my security when we were first married. There were times when she wanted to hold hands or wanted me to have my arm around her. But when that was not what she wanted, she was very clear about it. I often complained, "I never know what to do. I never know what you want!" Then I realized that listening, asking, and noticing weren't that difficult. As we grew in our communication, she got more comfortable about letting me know when she didn't want physical contact. I became more comfortable accepting her communication when I didn't make it about me. What initially seemed very threatening later became the communication I valued because it told me what she would enjoy at any given moment.

For the obsessive person, everything is about him or her. If the spouse doesn't respond in the desired way, the obsessive person experiences anger, rage, rejection, or some other negative emotional response. This very response proves that the actions were not for love, but for personal gratification. Obsession masks control with what looks like love.

Obsessive people do not recognize the difference between the need for love and the need for love from a specific person. In their minds this one person controls all of their future happiness. They have to have this person. When obsessive individuals realize they can't get what they want by doing acts of kindness, they change their strategy.

They may try better things, like buying jewelry, cars, or houses. When they do not see the "positive" efforts accomplish the task, though, they revert to negative behavior. And the negative behavior of obsessive people can quickly escalate from verbal to physical abuse.

The Issues of Obsession

Love does not have several different tactics. There is no plan B for the person who walks in love. If love is not enough, there is not another plan. Personally, I do not want what love does not accomplish.

Obsession masks control with what looks like love.

> *Love is patient, love is kind. It does not envy, it does not boast, it is not proud. It is not rude, it is not self-seeking, it is not easily angered, it keeps no record of wrongs. Love does not delight in evil but rejoices with the truth. It always protects, always trusts, always hopes, always perseveres.*
> (1 Corinthians 13:4–7 NIV)

Love does not have a dark side. When these characteristics of *agape*-love do not produce the desired results, love does not turn to any other method.

You see, love is a two-sided coin. It is equally nurturing and challenging. The person who walks in love is not afraid to challenge—but he never seeks to control. Love does not have personal gratification as its main objective. Love seeks mutual gratification. Even when the loving person has to confront or challenge, he or she does not withdraw support and nurturing. Neither is the motive of a challenge to bring more personal benefit. Rather, it is to benefit the other person as much as the relationship itself.

Obsessive people fear the possibility of their mates having a life beyond them. This would be one of the greatest threats imaginable. The pampered life the obsessive person offers is sometimes little more than payment for security. If you stay home you won't run the risk of meeting someone else. If I meet all of your needs you will love me and want me forever.

The obsessive person is the classic example of codependency. He or she is looking for someone or something on the outside to meet a need that only God can meet on the inside, in the heart.[22] It will never happen!

Besides the obvious codependency issues in obsession, there also is the issue of unrealistic expectations. Several years ago there was research done that discovered most American women have unrealistic expectations about marriage. American women tend to expect marriage and a mate to fulfill far more of their needs than European women expect. These expectations create an incredible amount of pressure for both husband and wife. They are very damaging to the relationship.

If you are expecting your marriage to be the solution to all of life's problems, you are at least peeking through the corridors that lead to obsession. Every person must have a life and identity beyond his or her mate. Do not make your mate the sum total of all your happiness. No one is capable of bearing such a weight. (If you walk in love, it can help you reveal and in some cases prevent obsessive tendencies from growing.)

Obsessive people have no dreams that can be fulfilled apart from the person they "need." But every person needs to have his or her own life-dream apart from a mate.

---

[22] For more on this topic, read *Escape from Codependent Christianity* (Huntsville, Alabama: Impact International Publication, 1997).

Together a husband and wife build a dream for their marriage. Both should share a dream of what they want their marriage to be. It is in the sharing of this dream where two become one. This shared dream is the life a couple builds together. Yet each must have a personal, individual life-dream.

The moment you factor someone else into your life-dream, you develop a belief that you cannot live your personal dream apart from your mate. This is the framework for many struggles and heartaches. If you ever believe you cannot live your personal dreams apart from your mate, you are a candidate for obsessive behavior. This is what leads many people into a lifetime of control. If a person can't live his or her dream without the spouse, then the spouse becomes more of a focus than the dream. That is too challenging for the obsessive person and too much pressure for the spouse.

Every person needs to have his or her own life-dream apart from a mate.

I am the pastor of Impact of Huntsville, our church. Brenda and I do not pastor the church together. She isn't called to pastor just because I am. I give her the freedom to live her dreams, and she gives me the freedom to live my dreams. Together we live our shared dream for our marriage. Neither of us has to give up our personal dreams for the other. Neither of us becomes responsible for the other's fulfillment. We bring fulfillment from the other areas of our lives into our relationship instead of letting the demands of our life-dream bring pressure to the relationship. Every place we find fulfillment apart from one another becomes a positive investment in our relationship. When we come together, it is not out of desperation. We are two fulfilled people sharing the fullness of our lives together.

Are you willing to let your mate have a personal life-dream that does not include you? Are you expecting your relationship to meet too many of life's needs? Are you committed to the fact that you can and will live your life-dream regardless of what your mate does? Do you impose your dreams onto your mate? Do you give your partner freedom to express his or her life-dreams? Are you masking obsessive control behind acts of kindness? The way you answer these questions will reveal what could be the beginning tendencies toward obsession. Find ways to make sure you and your mate have personal fulfillment outside of your relationship with one another. Make sure your marriage is not carrying the total weight of your life's happiness!

Chapter 22

Help! I'm Trapped

Chapter 22

Help! I'm Trapped

One of the greatest enemies to solving any of life's situations is the feeling of being trapped. This feeling sets off a series of emotional reactions that prevents people from solving problems on any level, but especially relational problems. One of those reactions is doing something because we "ought" to. However, we never experience grace to do what we "ought" to do; we experience grace to do what we desire to do. When people do the right things from an "ought to" attitude, they never produce the real fruit.

Anytime I hear the words *ought to, should,* or *need to* in my self-talk, I stop and ask myself, "Do I really want to do this? If so, why?" These phrases represent pressure from an outside source; they are indicators of beliefs forced on us by others or by our own faulty concepts and needs. Paul said, *"All things are lawful for me, but not all things are helpful; all things are lawful for me, but not all things edify"* (1 Corinthians 10:23 NKJV). He freed himself from the mere aspect of right and wrong, from the "ought to" mentality. He did not do things on the simple basis of right and wrong; he did things that were constructive and edifying. The result was a lifetime of wholehearted service to God.

In Galatians, Paul pointed out the incredible paradox of being free from being a servant while still being God's bondservant. In Galatians 4:7 he said, *"You are no longer a slave but a son, and if a son, then an heir of God through Christ"* (NKJV). Like the love servant of the Old Testament, Paul knew he had been freed from slavery. Yet his love for his Master and Redeemer was so great that he chose to spend his life in service to Him. Paul is the type of person God is looking for. God doesn't want people serving because they think they are obligated; He wants people to serve because they are in love with Him.

Obligation Destroys Love

This same emotional freedom should be the bond that holds our marriages together. It should not be the vows or the marriage license that keep us together, or a sense of obligation; it should be deep abiding love. Anything else will create feelings of obligation and bondage. People, like animals, become very dangerous when they feel trapped. Obligation will not force someone to love you. It will make him or her want to escape—sometimes violently!

> Deep abiding love and emotional freedom should be the bond that holds our marriages together.

Marriage, in a very paradoxical manner, is free enterprise. In other words, you can't make someone stay with you. If what you offer is not valuable enough, the other party may choose to leave. The church has used religious obligation as the motivation to make marriage work. The truth is, some Christian groups have a higher rate of divorce than non-Christian ones. I personally believe this forced obligation is at least part of the reason. It creates an emotional environment that destroys love and engenders hatred.

One of the first things I tell people who come in for marriage counseling is, "Both of you better realize that your mate is not obligated to stay. If you want this person in your life, you better give him or her good enough reasons to be there." Religious legalism takes what should be a commitment of love and turns it into bondage. This type of bondage falsely legitimizes much abuse. The logic is, "After all, you've got to stay!"

When a couple comes in for counseling and one of them is trying to use Scripture to obligate or force the other to stay, I know the marriage will probably end in divorce. This tactic may work for a while, but as one man told me, "If I have to live with her to go to heaven, I'd rather go to hell!"

When I can get a person to stop using God and the Bible as a means of controlling his or her mate, I can often help the couple recover love. I have never, however, in thirty years, ever seen love grow in an environment of obligation. I personally believe that a strong personal commitment to Jesus will move individuals to be open and flexible, but it can't make them have passionate, affectionate love.

In the book *Divorce Busting*, a secular counselor shares her discoveries about the pain of people who had made divorce their primary option. Early in her practice when couples came in who were not happy, she would encourage them to divorce. At some point she began to realize the incredible pain and suffering of those who opted for divorce without attempting to find real solutions. The majority of divorced people felt it would have been better to make their marriage work—even many who were in a successful second marriage! Almost all of them said they wished they had stayed and worked it out.[23] However, if a marriage is going to heal, it will heal because it is subjected to a godly process of free choices, personal responsibility, and *agape-love*. It can never heal because of obligation.

The Freedom to Let Go

When people stay in relationships because of obligation, it can become a breeding ground for deep hurt. Another thing I say to couples very early in marriage counseling is, "If either of you have no intention of working out these problems, say so now. There is no need to stay together and inflict pain on one another if you don't intend to work it out." When people do not intend to stay in a relationship, yet feel trapped, the only way to escape is if the other party decides to leave. And the only way to get the other person to leave is to force him or her out by cruelty and rejection. No one wins in this scenario. Yet religious obligation nourishes this kind of environment.

Marriage is a free enterprise. If what you offer is not valuable enough, the other party may choose to leave.

We have already discussed the sickness involved in need-oriented relationships. We've talked about obsession and control. None of these things causes a person to love you! If you are going to bring a Bible into the arena to save your marriage, do it by sitting down with your mate and acknowledging, "I know where I have failed, and I am accepting my responsibilities. I am trusting God to help me become a more loving man (or woman)."

---

[23] Michele Weiner-Davis, *Divorce Busting*, (New York: Simon & Schuster, 1993), 11–20.

Lazy, controlling people use obligation to get what they are not willing to inspire...commitment. They trap people and make them obligated through religion, pity, or fear. Obligation is a cop-out for those who don't want to put forth the effort to walk in love. These people don't want to accept personal responsibility to stimulate love. In their fear and self-centeredness, they fail to see that walking in love is the only way to restore lost love. In their obsession, they refuse to accept that the person who will not stay because of love should be let go!

It is this freedom to leave that keeps us challenged to keep love alive. It is this freedom that makes me want to be desirable. It is this freedom that moves Brenda to put forth the extra effort to make me feel loved when she really doesn't have to do so. This freedom never causes us to feel trapped or smothered; it makes us feel loved and valued.

I love my wife more than I ever knew I could love anyone, and I am committed to my marriage. Yet I have communicated to her in the most loving way that if our love doesn't hold us together, I would never want her to stay. That kind of communication creates high levels of personal responsibility. It also creates high levels of love and passion! Neither of us feel trapped. We feel loved.

Do you use the Bible to control your mate? Do you ever try to create obligation as a reason to stay together? Has your partner ever expressed feelings of being trapped? Are you willing to give your mate freedom of choice and then inspire love? If loving your spouse is not enough to make your spouse want to stay, are you willing to let him or her go?[24]

---

[24] This does not mean that I consider divorce to be the most viable option for reconciling differences. It means that I recommend love instead of obligation as the way to save a marriage.

Chapter 23

When the Damage Is Done

Chapter 23

When the Damage Is Done

I think one of the most tragic things I see is when a couple comes in for counseling and the damage has already been done. They long for what they once had. They are heart-broken. They want it to work, but they're afraid to trust, afraid of getting hurt again. They don't want to let go, yet they are afraid to hold on. They are too afraid to do what it takes to rebuild a loving relationship.

It is much more challenging to restore lost love than it is to get it the first time around. It sometimes can take years to overcome the damage that has been inflicted by self-centeredness, abuse, or neglect. Nevertheless, there are some things that can speed up the process of restoring lost love. It may take time, but it is much easier to invest several years than to face a painful divorce with all its subsequent, unavoidable results.

Speeding Up the Process

Realize you are starting over. Do nothing out of obligation. Expect nothing out of obligation. Commit your life to *agape-*love. Do whatever it takes to restore your sense of value and preciousness of your mate. Commit yourself to building a new relationship, and then do what it takes. Win your mate's love back the same way you won it the first time. Go on dates. Make life fun. Treat him or her special.

One of my children asked Brenda and I to watch her child on Friday night. Brenda kindly declined and said, "That's our date night." Someone commented, "You mean you couldn't get your mom to watch your kids?" Our daughter responded, "I just hope when I've been married that long that my husband still wants to date me."

Our dates consist of anything we decide to do. Sometimes it is dinner and a movie. Sometimes it is shopping. Occasionally we will go away for a couple of nights and stay in a motel. Earlier in our marriage when we couldn't afford a motel, we would take the kids to sitters and enjoy time at home alone. Just make sure it is something both of you will enjoy!

> Living in *agape*-love is impossible apart from experiencing the continual, stabilizing love of God.

Exercise safe communication. It is the way you will find the answers to your questions. Learn what makes your mate feel loved and make that a life priority. Above all, own "your stuff." Accept responsibility. Nothing derails one's attempts to rebuild trust like blame-shifting or denial.

Make life changes. Don't change what you do just to make your mate happy. That won't last long. As soon as you get what you want, you'll revert to your old ways. If necessary, get individual help. Don't wait for your mate to get counseling. Get what you yourself need to be a better person and you'll be a better husband or wife.

Renew your commitments to the Lord. Build a real relationship with Jesus that empowers you to walk in love. Living in *agape*-love is impossible apart from experiencing the continual, stabilizing love of God.

Restore your sex drive. When sexual desire is gone, do not assume it is purely relational. I have worked with many couples who assumed they were no longer in love simply because one of them had lost sexual desire for the other. Very often the problem is physical. More than once I have put someone on a simple herbal formula and restored the sex drive. Suddenly, the person was passionate about his or her mate again. Make sure you are not dealing with a physical problem. Implement some of the steps suggested in this book to create emotional triggers for sexual intimacy.

Look for all that you can value and appreciate about your mate. Make a list of all the reasons you wanted this relationship. Use the many techniques and suggestions that you have found in this book to keep love alive. Start capturing moments!

Press beyond the awkwardness. When rebuilding a relationship, awkwardness can be a huge obstacle. It is always uncomfortable offering affection and kindness when you are not sure how it will be received. Yet if you wait until it is one hundred percent safe, you'll probably never take the steps you need to take. Overcome the awkwardness, but don't be pushy. Learn to notice and be aware of your spouse's responses. Accept the fact that awkwardness is a part of the price we pay for our destructive past. When the response is not reciprocated, show love through patience.

Solve problems every day. When I was sixteen, I had a job selling vacuum cleaners door-to-door. One day the secretary who provided us with our leads told me that she and her husband made a promise when they got married that they would kiss good-night every night. That made an incredible impression on me. So I made it a part of my life plan. The problem with that commitment comes when you have unresolved issues. Then you don't want to kiss! The Bible tells us, *"Let not the sun go down upon your wrath"* (Ephesians 4:26). In order for Brenda and I to kiss good-night, we have to resolve our issues on a daily basis. Make sure that, when you go to bed, you can kiss good-night and enjoy it.

Keep the bond of love alive. Nothing bonds two people together as much as safe, genuine lovemaking. When couples go too long without making loving, an emotional distance grows between them. They lose touch with one another. Make love! Make it safe, enjoyable, and never forced. Only make love when both partners desire it. Just as powerfully as lovemaking can bind two people together, it also can drive them apart when it is not one hundred percent consensual.

Don't be afraid to love. All God requires of you is *agape*-love and a willingness to allow the other forms of love to grow. You have never been hurt by walking in *agape*-love. Being kind and patient does not mean you get used. It may simply mean that you are kind when you say no! It means you don't have to be angry or attack a person to disagree.

Love never brings pain. When there is pain, there are always other factors involved. Many people never restore love simply because they don't want to run the risks. Their false ideas about love are linked to many bad associations. But you must realize that refusing to love means that you are rejecting the basis of everything Jesus taught and stood for. He has nothing else to offer you for this life. He has no truth that will work in your life, unless it is based in love. You can't know God or even escape fear beyond your willingness to give yourself to a life of love. *"There is no fear in love; but perfect love casts out fear"* (1 John 4:18 NKJV).

Create a safe environment for the people around you. Make it safe for people to express themselves. Make it safe for people to say no. Let people see that, regardless of their actions, you are committed to the love of God. When people have nothing to gain or lose by our reactions, we discover the truth. When people become convinced of our love, they will be as open, honest, and responsive as they are capable of being.

Trust in the power of love. The Bible says, *"Love never fails"* (1 Corinthians 13:8 NKJV). Some research indicates that this could be translated as "love never ceases to be effective." Although other things and other approaches may fail to be effective, love never fails to be effective. If love doesn't work, nothing will. Nothing will win a person's heart like genuine love. Control and manipulation can give you a response, but the moment the threat is gone, you no longer have the desired response. And when you do get the desired response, there is always something lacking. If *agape*-love is not enough, nothing else is enough. You have hope as long as you are committed to love.

Let people see that, regardless of their actions, you are committed to the love of God.

Make a decision. Am I really willing to love? Do I believe that *agape*-love will get me what I desire in my relationships? Am I committed to walking in love regardless of how others react? Am I committed to making my mate feel precious, safe, and special? Am I investing in my relationship with God in such a way that I am developing godly character? These are decisions that will bring the grace of God to empower you to live a life of love and romance.

In Conclusion

As a child I longed for love so deeply it felt like a pain in the center of my being. Because of the emptiness of a broken, dysfunctional family, I wanted love so badly that I went out in codependent fashion and made every mistake, committed every sin, and hurt every relationship. It was hard for me to believe that I would ever find a love I wouldn't destroy. Yet today I am living the life that few believe exists and that even fewer have the courage to live. I'm in love.

When I tell people some of the sacrifices that Brenda and I have made, when I talk about how long it took for some of the changes to occur in our lives, they ask, "Was it worth it?" The pain that I experienced by having to grow up is nothing compared to the pain of a failed relationship. The pride that I had to swallow was like taking medicine that was bitter to the taste, but made me well.

Today Brenda and I have five kids and nine grandchildren. And we are in love. We have romance, passion, and excitement. My wife is my best friend. Just a few nights ago as we lay in bed holding one another, Brenda said, "I wish we had grown up together. I wish we had never wasted any of our lives." My reply was simple. "I feel like I'm seventeen and dating the girl of my dreams. It can't be any better than this."

As we have discussed many times, when we were young, we could not have had the kind of life we have today. We could not have faced the obstacles for which we didn't have tools to use. Today we do. And so do you.

Today, after reading this book, you have more tools than you did before. You now have many of the tools necessary to

start a healthy relationship. You now know how to recover lost love. You can find yourself in your twilight years still in love and still wanting to kiss the love of your life.

Yes, we still kiss...and it's getting better!

About the Author

Almost thirty years ago, James Richards found Jesus and answered the call to ministry. His dramatic conversion and passion to help hurting people launched him onto the streets of Huntsville, Alabama. His mission was to reach teenagers and drug abusers.

Before his salvation, James was a professional musician with all the trappings of a worldly lifestyle. More than anything, he was searching for real freedom. Sick of himself and his empty pursuits, he hated all that his life had become. He turned to drugs as a means of escape and relief. Although he was desperate to find God, his emotional outrage made people afraid to tell him about Jesus. He sought help but became more confused and hopeless than before. He heard much religious talk, but not the life-changing Gospel.

Through a miraculous encounter with God, James Richards gave his life to the Lord and was set free from his addictions. His whole life changed! Now, after years of ministry, Dr. Richards still believes there's no one God can't help, and there's no one God doesn't love. He has committed his life to helping people experience that love. If his life is a model for anything, it is that God never quits on anyone.

Dr. Richards—author, teacher, theologian, counselor, and businessman—is president and founder of Impact Ministries, a multifaceted, international ministry committed to helping those whom the church has not yet reached. He is on the cutting edge of what works in today's society. He is president and founder of Impact International School of Ministry, Impact International Fellowship of Ministers, Impact Treatment Center, Impact of Huntsville Church, and Impact International Publications. Thousands have been saved, healed, and delivered every year through his worldwide crusades and pastors' seminars.

With doctorates in theology, human behavior, and alternative medicine, and an honorary doctorate in world evangelism, Dr. Richards is also a certified detox specialist and drug counselor, as well as a trainer for the National Acupuncture Detoxification Association (NADA). His uncompromising yet positive approach to the Gospel strengthens, instructs, and challenges people to new levels of victory, power, and service. Dr. Richards' extensive experience in working with substance abuse, codependency, and other social/emotional issues has led him to pioneer effective, creative, Bible-based approaches to ministry that meet the needs of today's world.

More than anything else, Dr. Richards believes that people need to be made whole by experiencing God's unconditional love. His message is simple, practical, and powerful. His passion is to change the way the world sees God so that people can experience a relationship with Him through Jesus.

He and his wife, Brenda, have five daughters and nine grandchildren and reside in Huntsville, Alabama.

About Impact Ministries

James B. Richards is president of Impact Ministries. This multifaceted, worldwide organization is pioneering a ministry movement that is making an impact on the entire world. Impact Ministries is committed to providing relevant, meaningful ministry to all nations, while equipping a new breed of leaders who are prepared to meet the challenges of the new millennium. To meet this worldwide demand, the ministry consists of:

1. Impact of Huntsville, a vibrant, cutting-edge, local church based in Huntsville, Alabama
2. Impact International Ministries, the missions arm of the organization that reaches the nations of the world
3. Impact International Fellowship of Ministers, a worldwide ministry base that trains, equips, and serves ministers to live their call while pioneering a new level of leadership
4. Impact International Publications, changing the way the world sees God through books, audio, video, and other published materials
5. Impact Ministries, which conducts life-changing seminars and outreaches in North America
6. Impact International School of Ministry, which provides one of the most unique ministry training opportunities in the world

For information on these and other services provided by Dr. Richards and his ministry team contact us at:

3300 N. Broad Place
Huntsville, AL 35805
256-536-9402
www.impactministries.com

Other Books by James B. Richards

The Prayer Organizer	ISBN: 0-92474-801-X	108 pages
Grace: The Power to Change	ISBN: 0-88368-730-5	192 pages
The Gospel of Peace	ISBN: 0-88368-487-X	208 pages
How to Stop the Pain	ISBN: 0-88368-722-4	208 pages
Escape from Codependent Christianity	ISBN: 0-92474-810-9	214 pages
Leadership That Builds People Vol. 1	ISBN: 0-92474-806-0	160 pages
Leadership That Builds People Vol. 2	ISBN: 0-92474-811-7	165 pages
Satan Unmasked	ISBN: 0-92474-812-5	163 pages
Taking the Limits Off God	ISBN: 0-92474-800-1	87 pages
My Church, My Family	ISBN: 0-92474-809-5	153 pages
Supernatural Ministry	ISBN: 0-92474-814-1	222 pages

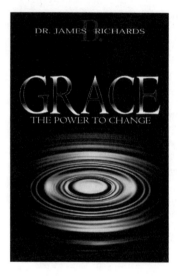

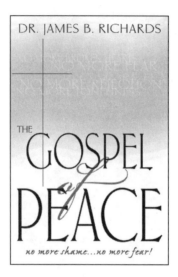